EASTERN STATE PENITENTIARY

*Crucible of
Good Intentions*

Eastern State Penitentiary

Crucible of Good Intentions

Norman Johnston

with Kenneth Finkel and Jeffrey A. Cohen

*Distributed by the
University of Pennsylvania Press*

*Philadelphia Museum of Art
for the Eastern State Penitentiary
Task Force of The Preservation Coalition
of Greater Philadelphia*

This book is published on the occasion of the exhibition "Eastern State Penitentiary at Fairmount: Crucible of Good Intentions" at the Philadelphia Museum of Art from July 16 to September 11, 1994.

The publication and exhibition were supported by a generous grant from The Pew Charitable Trusts.

Designed by Phillip Unetic with Meghan J. Alonzo

© 1994 Philadelphia Museum of Art
P.O. Box 7646, Philadelphia, Pennsylvania 19101-7646

Produced by the Department of Publications and Graphics
Edited by Jane Watkins with W. Douglass Paschall

Printed and bound in the United States of America

Library of Congress Cataloging-in-Publication Data

Johnston, Norman Bruce, 1921–
    Eastern State Penitentiary: crucible of good intentions / Norman Johnston, with Kenneth Finkel and Jeffrey A. Cohen.
        p. cm.
    ". . . Published on the occasion of an exhibition at the Philadelphia Museum of Art from July 16 to Sept. 11, 1994"–T.p. verso.
    ISBN 0-8122-7965-4
    1. Eastern State Penitentiary of Pennsylvania—History. 2. Haviland, John, 1792–1852—Criticism and interpretation. 3. Philadelphia (Pa.)—Buildings, structures, etc. 4. Architecture—Human factors—Pennsylvania—Philadelphia—History—19th century. 5. Quakers—Pennsylvania—Philadelphia—History—19th century. I. Finkel, Kenneth. II. Cohen, Jeffrey A., 1952– . III. Preservation Coalition of Greater Philadelphia. Eastern State Penitentiary Task Force. IV. Philadelphia Museum of Art. V. Title.
HV9475.P3E195 1994   94-21485
365'.974811—dc20   CIP

All rights reserved. No part of this publication may be reproduced, stored in a retrieval system, or transmitted in any form or by any means, electronic, mechanical, photocopying, recording, or otherwise, without prior permission, in writing, from the publisher.

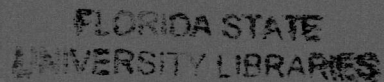

Contents

Preface   6
*Anne d'Harnoncourt
and Darrel Sewell*

I
Philadelphia in the 1820s:
A New Civic Consciousness   9
Kenneth Finkel

II
Reforming Criminals   21
Norman Johnston

III
Building the Ideal Prison   31
Norman Johnston

IV
Noble Ideas Collide with Reality   47
Norman Johnston

V
Cherry Hill: Model for the World   69
Norman Johnston

VI
Accommodation and Redefinition
in the Twentieth Century   81
Jeffrey A. Cohen

VII
The Legacy of Cherry Hill   101
Norman Johnston

Notes to the Text   106

Preface

This book and the accompanying exhibition celebrate the history, the architecture, and now the assured survival of Eastern State Penitentiary. A Philadelphia landmark from its beginnings in 1821, the penitentiary stands today as testimony to the social progress, the civic pride and activism, and the outstanding new architecture that distinguished Philadelphia in the 1820s.

The impetus for both the book and the exhibition came from the Eastern State Penitentiary Task Force, a spirited group of architects, museum curators, academics, preservationists, planners, leaders of neighborhood organizations, and members of the Pennsylvania Prison Society, who united to draw attention to the penitentiary as a masterwork by architect John Haviland and a key monument in the history of Philadelphia. Built in the remarkably dynamic period of social and architectural innovation in Philadelphia in the 1820s, the penitentiary remained in use until it was vacated in 1971. The Task Force, now a committee of The Preservation Coalition of Greater Philadelphia, was formed in 1988 to build a constituency for the derelict property and to find alternatives to plans to sell the penitentiary and its eleven-acre site for private development. Although the prison was registered as a National Historic Landmark in 1965, development schemes put forward for its reuse would have required substantial demolition of the buildings inside the perimeter walls.

Since 1988 the Task Force's activities have ranged from grass-roots efforts, such as lectures and the popular tours of the site to fund emergency building repairs, to long-range planning and advocacy for the preservation and sensitive reuse of the site. A 1988 grant from The Samuel S. Fels Fund allowed the compilation of archival information and a bibliography relating to the penitentiary and the establishment of a computer database. In October 1989 a national symposium was organized by the Task Force in collaboration with the National Trust for Historic Preservation to study options for a reuse plan that would require as little demolition as possible and allow both public access and revenue-producing components. The City of Philadelphia sponsored a comprehensive Building Condition Assessment in 1989 and a Protection and Stabilization Plan in 1990.

A grant from The Pew Charitable Trusts to The Preservation Coalition of Greater Philadelphia in March 1991 funded a program for comprehensive study of the prison, including a reuse model, a study of potential uses for the administration building, a site-operation study devoted to issues of management and marketing, an oral-history project, a complete historic structures report, as well as this publication and the accompanying exhibition. As the grant period draws to a close, the near-simultaneous appearance of these last three elements of the project signify the successful completion of the Task Force's first campaign for the protection and renewed appreciation of this extraordinary building. These efforts were ably coordinated by Milton Marks, Director of the Eastern State Penitentiary Project of The Preservation Coalition of Greater Philadelphia. Generous support has also come from the City of Philadelphia, the Claneil Foundation, Inc., The Getty Grant Program of the J. Paul Getty Trust, The Andy Warhol Foundation for the Visual Arts, CoreStates, and The Philadelphia Chapter of The American Institute of Architects.

This is the second time in recent years that the Philadelphia Museum of Art has prepared a publication and devoted an exhibition to an example of the architecture of civic idealism in Philadelphia during the 1820s. As the foundations were being laid for Eastern State Penitentiary in 1822 in the Fairmount section of the city, just a short distance away on the banks of the Schuylkill River a new waterworks, with machinery driven by water power, was put into operation to meet the growing city's need for an abundant supply of water. The Fairmount Waterworks, the subject of an exhibition and publication at this Museum in 1988, soon became one of the city's main attractions; the power and size of its waterwheels and pumps were engineering marvels, and its elevated site in open country was developed into a park to provide a refuge from the crowded city.

The delights of the waterworks, with its paths for strolling and vistas in the open air, spread out in dramatic contrast to the deliberately grim turrets and massive stone walls of the penitentiary. The prison was designed by Haviland to embody the Building Commissioners' instructions to "convey to the mind a cheerless blank indicative of the misery which awaits the unhappy being who enters within its walls." Yet visits to both were considered essential stops in their day for sightseers to Philadelphia, and they were widely influential as model public works.

The importance of Eastern State Penitentiary, the philosophical origins of its experimental penal reform, the development of Haviland's innovative radial plan—which was adapted for more than three hundred prisons worldwide—and its subsequent history until the building was closed in 1971, are detailed in this book. It represents decades of research by Dr. Norman Johnston, the distinguished expert on penology and Professor of Sociology at Beaver College in Glenside, Pennsylvania, and a founding member of the Task Force, with contributions by architectural historian Dr. Jeffrey A. Cohen and Kenneth Finkel, Curator of Prints at The Library Company of Philadelphia. For the production of this book, Dr. Johnston collaborated with Jane Watkins, Senior Editor in the Museum's Department of Publications and Graphics, and with the talented freelance designer Phillip Unetic.

Perhaps understandably, the landscape setting and picturesque neoclassical buildings of the waterworks lent themselves as subjects for art more often than did the somber walls of the penitentiary;

yet, civic pride in the penitentiary and its international renown ensured that it, too, would be depicted frequently in the numerous views of Philadelphia that appeared from the late 1820s. To select the range of material for the exhibition we have been fortunate to have Kenneth Finkel as guest curator. Mr. Finkel served as founding Chairman of the Eastern State Penitentiary Task Force in 1988. His familiarity with public and private collections of graphic art in the city, his detailed knowledge of Philadelphia's history, and his fervent commitment to the preservation not only of buildings but of the fabric of life and traditions in the city made him the ideal person to assemble this visual history in images and objects.

At the Museum, the exhibition's organization and implementation were overseen in the Department of American Art by Darrel Sewell, with assistance from Mike Hammer. Insurance and transportation were arranged by the office of the Registrar. The Conservation Department stabilized the ironwork displayed in the exhibition, and the installations staff ensured careful handling of all the objects. The perennial challenge of presenting an exhibition devoted to a work of architecture, without being able to import the building itself, was solved by the handsome models constructed by William Christensen.

This is the most recent of an informal series of Museum exhibitions devoted to architecture in Philadelphia, beginning with the 1973 retrospective of the work of Frank Furness and continuing in 1976 with the Bicentennial project *Philadelphia: Three Centuries of American Art*. Subsequent exhibitions included the project devoted to the Fairmount Waterworks in 1988; *Building the City Beautiful: The Benjamin Franklin Parkway and the Philadelphia Museum of Art* in 1989; and most recently the monumental survey of the achievement of Louis I. Kahn, organized by The Museum of Contemporary Art, Los Angeles, which had its inaugural showing in Philadelphia in 1991.

Each of these projects has brought the Museum staff and visitors into rewarding contact with a diverse and dedicated group of individuals united in their ardent desire to preserve Philadelphia's rich architectural heritage in all its forms, to promote and explain it, and to make it accessible to the public. With their generously shared information and advice, we also have had the pleasure of seeing further discoveries in the private collections, museums, libraries, archives, and storerooms that are unmatched resources for images and artifacts that vividly evoke Philadelphia's history. All the lenders have been most generous and helpful, but we would like to express special thanks to The Library Company of Philadelphia and the Historical Society of Pennsylvania, whose enthusiasm and unstinting participation have made this exhibition possible.

Anne d'Harnoncourt
The George D. Widener Director

Darrel Sewell
The Robert L. McNeil, Jr., Curator of American Art

Philadelphia in the 1820s: A New Civic Consciousness

Kenneth Finkel

"They are all heavy tasteless piles of red brick," wrote Englishman Isaac Weld of Philadelphia's public buildings.[1] Like many other visitors to the new United States capital in the 1790s, Weld found Philadelphia unimpressive to the eye. With only a few recently built exceptions, the city lacked formality in its architectural bearing. Visitors found brick, red brick, where they would have anticipated white columns, capitals, entablatures, and pediments. Those familiar with British and European capitals expected the city conceived as a "holy experiment" by Quakers in the 1680s to have joined the architectural mainstream after more than a century.

But Quaker Philadelphia had not yet joined the mainstream. The city's buildings seemed designed more to change minds than to turn heads. Quaker idealism was still prevalent in the 1790s; Weld and others appreciated some of the city's plainest edifices as examples of originality and leadership. At the Walnut Street Jail at Sixth and Walnut Streets, a "spacious building of common stone," Weld looked at the experiment attempted within. Imprisonment there was aimed not at punishment, but rather at the reform of the prisoner, a new and progressive idea. This building was more than a mere jail, Weld wrote, it "deserves the name of a penitentiary house."[2]

In a widely translated contemporary report entitled *Des Prisons de Philadelphie*, Duc François-Alexandre-Frédéric de la Rochefoucauld-Liancourt (1747–1827) lauded the same experiment, noting the influences of the Philadelphia Society for Alleviating the Miseries of Public Prisons. "The Quakers were the chief promoters of this softened system," he wrote. "Public labour, . . . mutilation, and . . . whipping" were outlawed.[3] In a pod of experimental cells built within the twenty-year-old prison, Philadelphians tried to succeed where previous reformers had failed. If the architecture was not ambitious, its philosophy was. If the building's appearance was not elegant, its purpose was.

I Crucible of Good Intentions

This national capital seemed indifferent, if not actually opposed, to architectural pretention. In fact, Philadelphians' objection to white facades for their public buildings and their preference for red brick lasted at least another century.[4] Plain materials and fine proportions were deemed sufficient for the State House, where the Declaration of Independence and the United States Constitution were honed into documents acceptable to the nation and admired by the world. Not that Philadelphians were indifferent to style. They simply preferred buildings to be serviceable and elegant in their simplicity—like good ideas.

For William Penn, Philadelphia resembled a far-flung garden suburb of London, with noble conceptual underpinnings. This settlement distinguished itself from the usual, quasi-military, colonial outposts supported by foreign investors. This "holy experiment," with its grid of a "greene Country Towne," was born of an idealism firmly held.[5] That was before the seventeenth century had given way to the eighteenth century, and Philadelphia had evolved into an American political and commercial center. From 1790 to 1800 the city found itself, if temporarily, the United States capital. Was the vision of the colonial founder still fresh, still useful in this new and larger context? How would plain, self-contained, red-brick Philadelphia meet its new, cosmopolitan calling? Would Quaker idealism have anything to offer nineteenth-century Philadelphians?

The first architect of the transition from red brick to white marble was Benjamin Henry Latrobe. When the British-born and trained architect could convince his patrons to pay for it, he sheathed his buildings in pristine white marble. Latrobe struck a long-lasting chord in his address to the Society of Artists in 1811, praising Philadelphia as the "Athens of the Western world."[6] But instead of calling for the remaking of the city in a newer vision, like Pierre-Charles L'Enfant had done for the District of Columbia, Latrobe stepped back to honor and even embrace William Penn's original vision, claiming that Philadelphia would always benefit from Penn's wisdom and policy. The community had inherited Penn's "simplicity of . . . manners and principles," traits that would improve "the character of the whole population."[7]

Philadelphians in the early nineteenth century had two parallel missions: to redefine the city as a metropolis by creating an "Athens of the Western world" and to complete Penn's vision. The engine for change was Philadelphia's unprecedented growth. Beginning the century with nearly 68,000 residents in the city proper and 81,000 in Philadelphia County, the population swelled to 136,635 inhabitants by 1820. That figure would nearly double by 1840 and more than double again by 1860, when the county population stood at 565,000.[8] This completely transformed city, this proud metropolis, would soon re-articulate its identity in scores of events, institutions, publications, and, of course, new public architecture. By the end of the 1820s, Philadelphia had been remade into the largest, most economically secure, most socially responsible, and most culturally exciting city in the United States.

Penn's original intention for a river-to-river city had long been anticipated but long deferred. In the eighteenth century, Philadelphia had evolved as an urban crescent hugging the Delaware River in a northern and southern sprawl, extending well beyond the city limits. A port-based economy had dictated this development, which was often dense and unpleasant. For all its commercial activity, Water Street, east of Front Street, was "narrow and disagreeable to walk in," according to one observer.[9] Penn's intentions were for a more symmetrical, regular, town plan: "Settlers should improve the lots on the Schuylkill front, as soon as those on that of [the] Delaware; and by spreading towards the middle-ground, have made nearly equal progress towards the center, or Broad-street."[10] In order for this spreading to take place, two major forces were necessary: an industrial economy based upon portable sources of power and a rising population. Early-nineteenth-century Philadelphia had both.

By 1805 the Schuylkill River was bridged at Market Street, the main east-west axis of Penn's plan. The covered, wooden Permanent Bridge was originally intended to bear allegorical figures of Commerce and Agriculture, features from Philadelphia's coat of arms.[11] The bridge finally completed the vision of William Penn and his surveyor, Thomas Holme, and inspired a new burst of self-confidence. "Since the visits of the Yellow Fever," wrote an anonymous contributor to *The Portfolio* magazine in 1809, "the building tide has flowed westward with new and wonderful force, and the completion of the market between the two rivers will probably take place in the present generation."[12] This writer envisioned a river-to-river string of market shambles. Its brick piers and plastered, arched ceilings, a full two miles long, would be broken in the middle by Benjamin Henry Latrobe's pump house and terminated by the new Permanent Bridge. Although the markets never developed further west than Eighth Street, except for a small stretch west of Centre Square from Fifteenth to Seventeenth Streets, Philadelphia did spread from the Delaware River to the Schuylkill River by mid-century, a reality generally foreseen by the 1830s.[13]

A city growing fast needs constantly to renew its infrastructure, and Philadelphians did their best to keep up with the exploding metropolis by reinventing an array of support systems. Predictably, projects were often obsolete as soon as they were completed, sometimes even before. Latrobe's pump house, at Centre Square (where Philadelphia's City Hall is today), began supplying potable water in 1801, but was replaced by Frederick C.

Philadelphia in the 1820s: A New Civic Consciousness

After Thomas Holme (1624–1695), Detail of *The City Philadelphia: A Mapp of ye Improved Part of Pensilvania in America*, c. 1700. Sold by Geo. Willdey, London. Engraving, 16⅝ x 21¾" overall. The Library Company of Philadelphia.

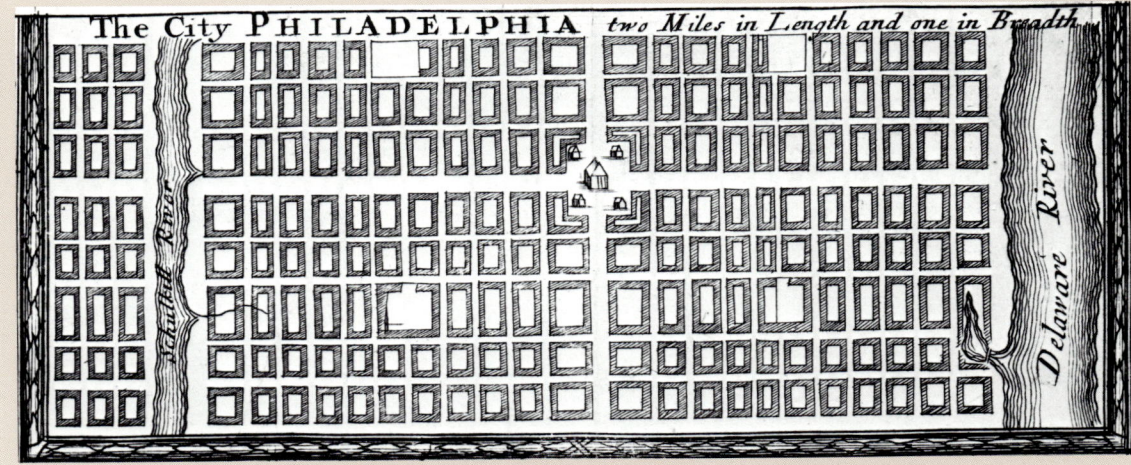

William Russell Birch (1755–1834) and Thomas Birch (1799–1851), *High Street, From the Country Marketplace Philadelphia*, 1798. Engraving and etching, 8¼ x 11⅛". The Library Company of Philadelphia.

I Crucible of Good Intentions

Launch of the U.S. Ship Pennsylvania, 1839. Wood engraving, 2½ x 4". From *A History of Philadelphia, with a Notice of Villages in the Vicinity* (Philadelphia: Daniel Bowen, 1839).

Graff's Fairmount Waterworks, begun in 1812. Latrobe's building stood idle until the end of its short existence, in 1828.[14]

"Our good city of Philadelphia—In twenty years the Manchester and Lyons of America," toasted the lawyer Pierre S. DuPonceau in 1829.[15] Commercial shipping was no longer the key to economic success, although vessels still plied from Philadelphia to Canton and Calcutta, and the city turned from shipping to shipbuilding. It took workers at the Navy Yard, then at the foot of Washington Avenue, fifteen years to build the world's largest man-of-war: the U.S.S. *Pennsylvania*. America's most heavily armed vessel featured a figurehead of Hercules in lionskin, armed with a club, by sculptor John Rush.[16] Such was the upbeat, proud tone of local industry, which, besides ships, produced chandeliers and carpets, sugar and saws. One-quarter of the nation's steel production would soon be Philadelphia-based and 45 percent of all American locomotives would come from the Baldwin factory at Broad and Spring Garden Streets.

Yet for all this growth and dramatic transformation, the city was steadily eclipsed by New York, whose population, and then economy, surpassed Philadelphia's. If economic prospects still seemed rosy throughout the 1820s, the stinging news came in 1831: New York State's economic growth was actually double that of Pennsylvania.[17] Within another two years, the Second Bank of the United States, originally chartered by the federal government in 1816, and ensconced on Chestnut Street near Fourth Street in a distinguished, classical, white marble temple by architect William Strickland, had begun its decline toward failure. No single building in the city of the 1820s stood so fully for Philadelphia's newfound self-confidence and former status as the nation's capital. No single building in the city of the 1830s became so poignant an emblem of the city's sudden reversal of fortune.

President Andrew Jackson had no intention of rechartering the bank and continuing the reign of the young, talented, and aristocratic Philadelphia banker Nicholas Biddle. In 1832, when the rechartering issue was in "Old Hickory's" hands, he visited Philadelphia (for medical reasons) and stayed in the United States Hotel, just opposite the bank. The serious, worldly facade must have rankled Jackson, who ordered a withdrawal of deposits in 1833. Nine years later Charles Dickens commented on the "mournful ghost-like aspect" of the building, a condition wholly blamed on Jackson. No one could have guessed that the city's fortunes would turn so far so fast, that its temple of finance would become a "Great Catacomb of investment."[18]

Despite this setback, the sharply rising population led to a boom in institutional construction. In fresh air, on open and affordable land surrounding an ever-expanding city core, grew an array of new philanthropic, penal, educational, and medical facilities. The Friends Asylum near Frankford, to the northeast, was considered to be far from the city, but even institutions closer in, such as the Orphan Asylum, at Eighteenth and Cherry Streets, or the Pennsylvania Institution for the Deaf and Dumb, built at Broad and Pine Streets, were, in 1824, outside the developed portion of the city. In a broad ring around the city (to the

Samuel Honeyman Kneass (1806–1858), *Second Bank of the United States at Philadelphia*, c. 1824. Watercolor, 10 x 17¼". The Library Company of Philadelphia.

north, west, and south) were a string of institutions: the House of Refuge, Girard College for Orphans, the Pennsylvania Hospital for the Insane, the Alms House, the United States Naval Asylum, and Moyamensing Prison. All of these were large in scale and, for their time, progressive in nature. Yet none was so ambitious and so large as the Commonwealth's new Eastern State Penitentiary built on the gentle rise of land called Cherry Hill, just northeast of Fairmount.

At the same time, the cultural life of the city expanded dramatically with the rebuilding of the Chestnut Street Theatre, west of Sixth Street, by William Strickland (in 1822, after a fire of 1820). The all-new Arch Street Theatre, also by Strickland, opened in 1826. Thespians trod the boards and audiences filled the boxes of the Walnut Street Theatre at Ninth Street, remodeled by John Haviland in 1828. In addition to the standard imported fare, local playwrights were occasionally featured. The imminent opening of Eastern State Penitentiary served as fodder for one of Robert Montgomery Bird's "rascals" in an 1828 play set in Philadelphia entitled *The City Looking Glass*. The character Ringfinger offers tongue-in-cheek advice to his companion: "Whenever any body is disposed to kill you, cry *Penitentiary!* and he's off in a hurry."[19] The local fascination was also apparent to foreign visitors. "It requires more interest to get hanged, than to be made Governor of the State," wrote John M. Duncan ten years earlier.[20]

A measure of the pride in their optimistic city and its new institutions is

I CRUCIBLE OF GOOD INTENTIONS

the sudden increase of Philadelphia views published in the late 1820s. Not since the publication of Birch's views in 1800 (and a second edition in 1804) had the city been so extensively featured graphically. Samuel C. Atkinson's new monthly variety magazine, *The Casket*, featured four Philadelphia wood engravings published in 1827, including one of Eastern State Penitentiary that served as a source for the watercolorist David Johnston Kennedy. Before 1832, forty-five views of Philadelphia appeared in *The Casket*. Cephas Grier Childs published twenty-five in *Philadelphia and Its Environs* from 1827 to 1830, and Thomas Porter published thirty-three in *Picture of Philadelphia* of 1831. More than one hundred views in four years documented, if not celebrated, according to Childs, "the successful fulfillment of [Philadelphia's] original design."[21]

Events of the 1820s characterized the city's new pride and historical consciousness. Not since the Grand Federal Procession in 1788 had the city created such a spectacle as was seen on March 15, 1821. Nearly the entire population lined the city's streets and witnessed a grandiose Procession of Victuallers leading a record number of prizewinning cattle, oxen, hogs, sheep, kids, bear cubs, and fawns—all to slaughter.

Three and a half years later, the city had another occasion to celebrate, when the Marquis de Lafayette returned. In 1777 Lafayette had accompanied Gen. George Washington to Philadelphia. Nearly fifty years later, when Lafayette came back, the city made a spectacle of it. Traveling from New York, Lafayette stayed a night in Frankford and then proceeded down Fourth Street through elaborately painted arches to Independence Hall on September 28, 1824. As his entourage arrived, the frigate *John Adams* fired a salute from the Delaware River. "Lafayette Day" was followed by a week of receptions, balls, banquets, and meetings evoking and glorifying Revolutionary successes. According to Childs, "the Hall of Independence . . . was appropriated as his drawing room . . . presenting to the eye, the memory, and the feelings, a combination, animating and interesting beyond the power of language to express."[22] This popular event set the precedent for a parade celebrating Washington's Centennial in 1832, when Independence Hall was again

Edward Williams Clay (1799–1857), *The Downfall of Mother Bank*, 1833. Lithograph, 8⅜ x 13⅜". The Library Company of Philadelphia.

14

Philadelphia in the 1820s: A New Civic Consciousness

House of Refuge, Philadelphia, 1829. Wood engraving, 3 x 6⅜". From *Atkinson's Casket*, vol. 4, 1829.

Pennsylvania Hospital for the Insane, c. 1860. Engraving, 4⁵⁄₁₆ x 7⁷⁄₁₆". The Library Company of Philadelphia.

I CRUCIBLE OF GOOD INTENTIONS

Augustus Kollner (1813–1906), *United States Naval Asylum*, 1847. Watercolor, 9⅞ x 14". The Library Company of Philadelphia.

John Caspar Wild (c. 1804–1846) and John Collins (n.d.), *Moyamensing Prison, Philadelphia*, 1838. Lithograph, 5¼ x 7". From *Panorama and Views of Philadelphia and Its Vicinity* (Philadelphia: J. C. Wild and J. B. Chevalier, 1838).

Philadelphia in the 1820s: A New Civic Consciousness

David Johnston Kennedy (1816/17–1898), *Eastern Penitentiary, Coats Street, Philadelphia, founded in May 1823*, c. 1840. Watercolor, 6¾ x 10⅛". The Historical Society of Pennsylvania. After the engraving *A Correct View of Eastern State Penitentiary*, published in *Atkinson's Casket*, vol. 2, 1827.

a destination, this time for fifteen thousand marchers and floats, led by a corps of muscular men in white frocks and leather caps, bearing axes.[23]

In this expanding city of new ideas, new wealth, and new ambitions arose new tensions, and satire developed into an art. In 1819 Robert Waln, Jr., had taken aim at the fashionable set in his book *The Hermit in America*:

No sooner is one of our Philadelphia exquisites completely equipped, pads on his breast and shoulders, corsets around his waist, and plaits on his hips, to say nothing of the precise rotundity of that part of his collar over-topping his cravat;—no sooner is all this effected, and before the purlieus of Chesnut-street have been perambulated even for the ninetieth and ninth time; nay, even before his brother cronies have admired his exquisiteness,—the fashion changes.[24]

Edward Williams Clay, a lawyer who turned from bar to barb, used fashion to drive home his point. In a series of etchings of 1829, titled "Life in Philadelphia," Clay contrasted African Americans and Quakers, and mocked both minorities. One etching depicts a stylishly dressed African American woman ensconced in a lavish Empire parlor reading the florid dialect of a love letter. In Clay's interpretation of Quaker courtship, two Friends sit stiffly on plank chairs before a wooden mantle in an otherwise empty room. "Behold thou art fair Deborah, yea pleasant!" declares the male suitor. "Turn away thine eyes from me, Timothy, for they overcome me," answers his companion, "thy hair is as a flock of goats that appear from Gilead!"[25]

Philadelphia's new and sometimes jagged edges of the 1820s were softened by a popular antiquarian spirit. Lafayette's 1824 visit inspired the formation of

I CRUCIBLE OF GOOD INTENTIONS

The Walk in Chesnut Street, 1819. Etching with watercolor, 3⅜ x 6¼". From Robert Waln, Jr., *The Hermit in America* (Philadelphia: M. Thomas, 1819). The Library Company of Philadelphia.

Joseph Yeager (c. 1792–1859) after John Lewis Krimmel (1786–1821), *The Procession of Victuallers, at Fourth and Chestnut Streets*, 1821. Aquatint and etching with watercolor, 14⅜ x 23¾". Philadelphia Museum of Art. Gift of the estate of Charles M. B. Cadwalader.

Cephas Grier Childs (1793–1871) after George Strickland (1797–1851), *State House*, 1828. Engraving, 3 x 5". From *Views in Philadelphia and Its Environs, from Original Drawings Taken in 1827–30* (Philadelphia: C. G. Childs, 1827–30).

the Historical Society of Pennsylvania. John Fanning Watson collected and recorded memories of elderly citizens, accounts of buildings demolished, and even scraps of the gowns worn at the Meschianza Ball in 1778, distilling all this into the 740-page *Annals of Philadelphia, Being a Collection of Memoirs, Anecdotes, & Incidents of the City and Its Inhabitants*, first published in 1830. Watson's most impassioned pleas concerned protection for "discovered" sites that he and others considered especially historic. Europeans regularly protect places with powerful associations, Watson argued. "Who can . . . estimate . . . [the] value . . . of so much brick and mortar!" He pleaded that they be rescued and preserved: "There is a generation to come who will be grateful."[26] History bore out Watson's words. Despite Philadelphia's continued transformation through the nineteenth and early twentieth centuries, the city's origins remained the subject of intense interest. In the century after its publication, Watson's *Annals* was expanded and reissued twenty-eight times.

The attitudes that emerged in the 1820s concerning the value of the city's past guided generations of historians, collectors, and preservationists. This was a dramatic reversal of the approach of the 1810s, when (in 1813) the original wings of the State House were demolished and (in 1816) the original paneling in the Assembly Room was torn out and discarded. The tower had been removed years before, and the new changes resulted in a particularly uninspiring appearance for the most important historic building in the city, if not the nation. But in the 1820s, the city reversed its course and undertook a project to renovate and restore the State House. In 1828 Strickland designed a new wooden steeple. And in 1831 Haviland was commissioned to restore "to its ancient form" the Assembly Room, where the Declaration of Independence and the Constitution had been signed.[27]

By the 1820s Philadelphia had grown closer to Penn's vision. It had adopted a new image, a new public architecture. In this brief period when the responsibilities of Philadelphia as the nation's first capital had not yet completely faded and the influence of the city as the nation's financial center had not yet waned, Penn's town had blended the best of the new architectural professionalism and its civic idealism. When a New York editor commented that "the best architectural taste in the country is found at Philadelphia, as her public buildings make manifest,"[28] the writer was complimenting the work of John Haviland. And in Haviland's work, as in all of Philadelphia's architecture of the 1820s, nothing surpassed the scale, ambition, and design of Eastern State Penitentiary.

Reforming Criminals

NORMAN JOHNSTON

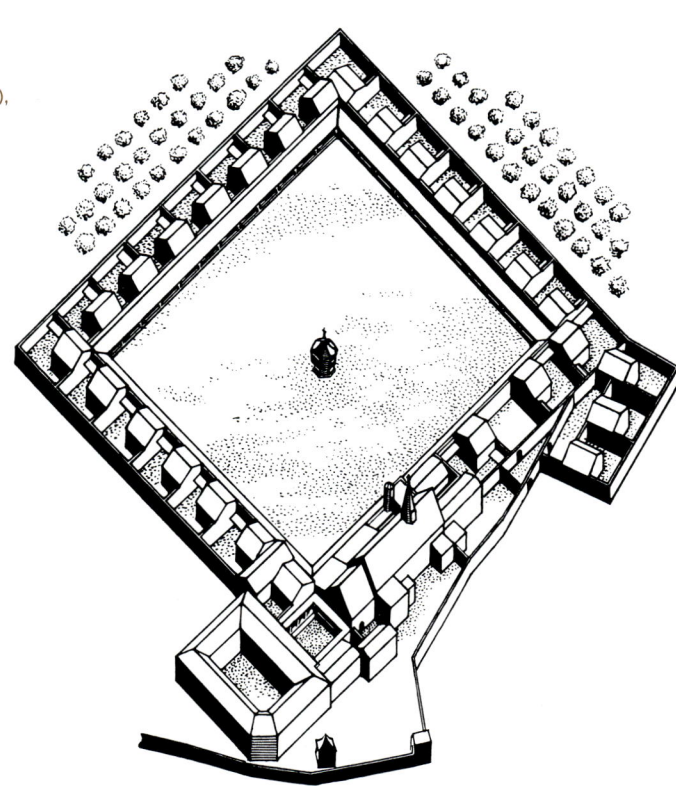

Mount Grace Charterhouse (the London Charterhouse), a fourteenth-century English monastic establishment where each monk was provided a small house and garden plot.

Traveling in the United States to study the criminal justice system in 1831, Alexis de Tocqueville wrote to his sister-in-law describing Philadelphia as a city "infatuated...with the penitentiary system."[1] To understand this only slightly exaggerated observation, we must look to the beginnings of the colony of Pennsylvania, and even earlier in Europe, to the first uses of imprisonment as punishment. William Penn and other early Philadelphia Quakers opposed the severe corporal and capital punishment applied in Britain, and considered imprisonment to be an effective alternative. Penn himself had been incarcerated in 1670 in England for his Quaker views, but because of his high social status had been confined to an inn rather than to a common jail, a benign punishment quite different from the treatment characteristic in English prisons. The penal code Penn adopted for the colony in 1682 therefore declared the offender's reform to be more important than his punishment and, for most crimes, substituted imprisonment for the death penalty or corporal punishment.

Early Uses of Imprisonment

The sentence of imprisonment instead of more sanguinary punishments was not a firmly established practice in the 1680s. Although prior to trial, execution, or banishment to a penal colony, the accused had always been confined in prisons, the idea of imprisonment used as punishment had only gradually come into favor, first by the Christian church for those under its direct jurisdiction and later by civil authorities for minor offenders.

Because of the large number of men and women in the medieval ecclesiastical bureaucracy, the church developed an independent system of adjudication and punishment. Consonant with the Christian doctrine of redemption, and as a result of the prohibition against the death penalty and most forms of corporal punishment common in the civil courts, the church viewed imprisonment, usually in isolation, as an instrument that would

CRUCIBLE OF GOOD INTENTIONS

punish and, it was believed, modify sinful or disruptive behavior.

As early as 817 a Benedictine council at Aix-la-Chapelle (Aachen) ruled that each monastery should provide for offenders a separate habitation, heated and with an attached workroom. Separation was not always feasible, however, and later church councils complained that, because of mingling, some prisoners were being adversely affected by others. Jean Mabillon, a Benedictine monk, writing around 1690, suggested that

penitents might be secluded in cells . . . and there employed in various sorts of labor. To each cell might be joined a little garden, where, at appointed hours, they might take an airing and cultivate the ground. They might, when assisting in public worship, be placed in separate stalls. . . . No visitors from the outside should be admitted; but the solitude of prisoners' lives should be unbroken, except by the visits of the Superior or some person deputed by him to exhort and console them.[2]

As isolation was central to various monastic orders, in many cases a monk's own cell could be used for punitive confinement by order of the abbot, who would specify the term's duration according to the seriousness of the infraction. At Mount Grace Charterhouse in England, for example, a small aperture in the wall of each monk's quarters allowed the passage of food and work materials to the occupant without social contact. In other monastic communities, special rooms were constructed, sometimes below ground. For extremely serious crimes, the offender was confined in a cell for life, and allowed virtually no contact with anyone.

In contrast, civil courts seldom used imprisonment as punishment before its first systematic employment in sixteenth-century houses of correction in the Netherlands.[3] Secular authorities customarily imprisoned men and women in common rooms converted from fortresses or castles, or later in jails and prisons built specifical-

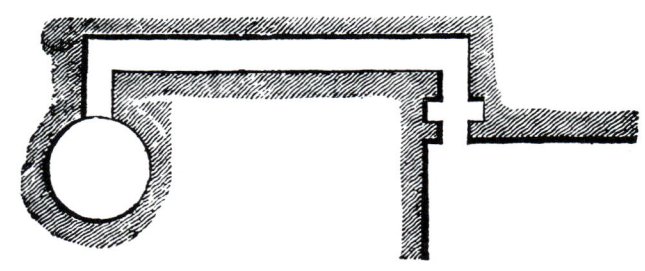

An underground cell used for confinement at Ewenny, a Benedictine establishment in England. From Richard Taylor, *Index Monasticus* (London: R. and A. Taylor, 1821).

A table of fees charged by the jailer of the Winchester County Jail, England, for various services in the 1770s.

Attributed to George Cruikshank (1792–1878), *Newgate—Prison Discipline, City of London System*, c. 1818. Engraving. Frontispiece to Joseph Adshead, *Prisons and Prisoners* (London: Longman, Brown, Green, and Longman, 1845).

ly as such.[4] Confinement at rigorous, productive labor began to supplant corporal punishment, exile, or execution for a variety of crimes, especially minor ones such as petty theft, prostitution, vagabondage, disorderly conduct, and what we now define as juvenile delinquency.

Prison Conditions and Reform

By the latter part of the eighteenth century, large numbers of men, women, and even children were held in prisons, sometimes together. Prisoners usually lived under conditions of incredible squalor and filth, frequently in underground dungeons. If the jail was small or insecure, inmates would be chained to the floor or wall. In many jails there was no provision for feeding the prisoners; they relied on charity or begged through the windows. Beds and bedding were seldom provided, and even in winter there was no heat. Investigating prison conditions in England, Elizabeth Fry (1780–1845), a Quaker, found 120 female prisoners confined in one room, openly drinking alcohol and sleeping on a bare floor.[5] Usually there were no facilities for bathing or washing clothes, and open sewers or privies were common. In such unsanitary conditions, vermin and communicable diseases were frequent hazards, the most deadly being "gaol fever," probably typhus.

A jailer might derive his income entirely from fees charged to inmates for various services: the removal of their chains, release from jail, and the provision of food, beds and bedding, or a private chamber. The jailer also made money

from the sale of liquor. If newcomers had no funds, some of their clothing would be taken and pawned in lieu of payment.

In contrast, prisoners with sufficient money could live in relative comfort, eat at the jailer's table, leave the prison from time to time, or even reside nearby. They might also have their spouses and children with them, or perhaps a prostitute. Those who could afford it were often given considerable freedom to pursue amusements. One observer described the diversions witnessed on a visit to a London prison in 1776:

I mentioned the billiard-table. They also play in the yard at skittles, mississippi [a card game], fives, tennis, &c. And not only the Prisoners: I saw among them several butchers and others from the market; who are admitted here as at another public house. The same may be seen in many other Prisons where the Gaoler keeps or lets the tap. Besides the inconvenience of this to Prisoners; the frequenting a Prison lessens the dread of being confined in one. On Monday night there was a Wine-Club: on Thursday night a Beer-Club: each lasting usually till one or two in the morning. I need not say how much riot these occasion; and how the sober Prisoners are annoyed by them.[6]

Prison conditions nevertheless attracted little attention in England, except from the Quakers. The Friends acquired a powerful ally when, in 1773, John Howard (1726–1790) became sheriff of Bedfordshire and was thus nominally responsible for the county jail. Earlier, Howard had been briefly held prisoner by French forces, and in his new post, he took a great interest in the physical conditions in his county's prisons. At his own expense, he made four trips through England, Wales, Ireland, and Scotland, and seven tours of the Continent, to inspect prisons. Departing from the theoretical nature of most contemporary writings about prisons, Howard objectively gathered specific details about diet, living conditions, staffing, regulations, and buildings in the first systematic prison survey ever conducted. He published his observations in a series of books beginning in 1777.[7]

In his travels, Howard saw a few exemplary institutions, most notably San Michele, a juvenile prison in Rome; a Belgian house of correction at Ghent; and the workhouses in Amsterdam. His experiences led him to conclude that it was essential for "all prisoners to have separate rooms; for hours of thoughtfulness and reflection are necessary." But he recognized the potential hazards of isolation, adding: "It should therefore be considered by those who are ready to commit, for a *long* term, petty offenders to *absolute* solitude, that such a state is more than human nature can bear."[8] Howard proposed the regimen of confinement to cells and work in silence, with liberal doses of religious instruction, that he had observed in the prison in Rome. He argued that proper architecture could enhance the surveillance of prisoners and guards, provide better ventilation, and improve sanitation; better management would result in greater control over guards as well as inmates and the elimination of fees charged by jailers.

What was the result of Howard's revelations? After the initial commotion had passed, virtually nothing. Prison reform in England was eventually forced by two unrelated events: the increasing ravages of gaol fever, which also killed judges, lawyers, jury members, and keepers; and the loss of the American colonies, where, in preceding decades, serious offenders had been sent in penal servitude. In the first years following the American Revolution, prisoners who previously would have been transported to Virginia or Georgia were instead confined in hulks, prison ships moored in rivers or harbors. Even after the establishment of penal colonies in Australia and New Zealand, there was increasing pressure to build new penitentiaries in England.

Gaol fever, the scourge of old prisons, was thought to be caused by miasmas; reformers reasoned that new prisons would have to be properly situated and designed for optimum circulation of air.[9] A clean water supply, effective drainage, adequate ventilation, and a proper diet would also do much to keep prisoners healthy. To stem disorder, corruption, and disease, inmates would be housed in separate cells and classified by gender, age, and seriousness of offense, all under the eye of the governor or warden. Productive labor, as had been initiated in several Dutch and German correctional institutions, would be required of all prisoners.

Some reformers favored solitary confinement with labor and religious instruction, as had been suggested by Howard, and occasionally officials attempted to establish such a system. Sir George O. Paul was the most influential British innovator in this regard; in 1791 at his Houses of Correction for Gloucestershire there was a small structure with fifty-two night cells and an equal number of day cells for work. At nearby Reading, inmates exercised alone in walled yards attached to each cell. None of these reforms was practiced for long or on a large scale, however, as overcrowding soon put an end to these and other experiments in Britain. Certainly none was attempted in a properly designed prison following a carefully thought-out philosophy. By 1816, at the very time that the State of Pennsylvania was considering isolation as punishment, county after county in Britain had phased out their unsuccessful programs of solitary confinement.

The new institutions had further proved to be an enormous burden on British taxpayers—in the 1790s in Gloucestershire, over 60 percent of the entire county budget was spent on prisons—and there was a hardening of attitudes about innovative and expensive prison reforms. Not only were objections raised about its cruelty and inhumanity,

Title page of the fourth edition of John Howard, *The State of the Prisons in England and Wales* (London: Printed for J. Johnson, C. Dilly, and T. Cadell, 1792).

Mather Brown (died 1831), *Portrait of John Howard*. Oil on canvas, 27¾ x 23". National Portrait Gallery, London.

THE
STATE
OF THE
PRISONS
IN
ENGLAND AND WALES,

WITH

PRELIMINARY OBSERVATIONS,

AND AN ACCOUNT OF SOME

FOREIGN PRISONS AND HOSPITALS.

BY JOHN HOWARD, F.R.S.

Ah little think the gay ——————
Whom pleasure, power, and affluence surround,
How many pine in want, and dungeon-glooms;
Shut from the common air.
            THOMSON.

THE FOURTH EDITION.

LONDON:
PRINTED FOR J. JOHNSON, C. DILLY, AND T. CADELL.
M DCC XCII.

Crucible of Good Intentions

as Howard had foreseen, but its workability was also questioned. In such inadequate facilities, inmates had found ways to circumvent their isolation and to communicate with one another. Inevitably there arose doubts about the very possibility of reform itself. A House of Commons committee in 1828 speculated whether the success of reformers in ridding prisons of the terrors of filth and disease had not compromised their deterrent value. Was prison life becoming too pleasant?

**America's First Penitentiary:
A Philosophy of Treatment Evolves**

Although the innovations that had been instituted under William Penn were largely eliminated by conservative interests in Britain and Pennsylvania following his death, the Quaker concern for the well-being of prisoners was never abandoned. In fact, in Philadelphia in the last quarter of the eighteenth century, the city's elite were increasingly active in prison matters. In spite of political tensions between Britain and her North American colonies, European and American penological reformers exchanged ideas through visits, books, and private correspondence.

Soon they would be able to test their theories. Overcrowding and disorderly behavior not unlike that found in English prisons characterized Philadelphia's Old Stone Prison, on the corner of Third Street and what is now Market Street, and prompted construction of a new prison, the Walnut Street Jail, in 1773.[10] Opposite the yard of the State House (Independence Hall), it was designed by one of the most prominent architects in the colonies at the time, Robert Smith, and opened when only partially finished, in 1776. The plan was traditional, consisting of a front building of three stories, flanked by two wings attached at right angles. As in British prisons of the period, inmates were housed together in large rooms. Aside from a handsome Georgian facade, which might have graced a city hall or a university building, the only architectural feature worthy of note was the use of brick vaulting to support the upper floors, making the building one of the earliest examples of relatively fireproof construction in colonial America.

In 1776 a group of influential Philadelphians formed an organization to assist local prisoners, especially by collecting food. After the war, spurred by the plight of the inmates in the Walnut Street Jail, Quakers and other local leaders created the Philadelphia Society for Alleviating the Miseries of Public Prisons, later called the Pennsylvania Prison Society, undoubtedly the first such organization in the world. Bishop William White, rector of Christ Church, presided over the new organization, made up of attorneys, merchants, and four physicians, including Benjamin Rush.

Members of the Prison Society were aware of penal reforms in the English counties, and kept abreast of new prison designs and the few early attempts to combine solitary confinement and labor.[11] The Prison Society was thoroughly familiar with Howard's work—copies of his books were in the private libraries of many Philadelphia reformers—and had corresponded with him on at least one occasion. Prison Society members also had contacts with the outstanding British penal figures Thomas Fowell Buxton, William Roscoe, and Joseph Gurney, with Charles Lucas of France, and with a number of Russian philanthropists. Benjamin Franklin and Thomas Jefferson brought back information about penal developments in Europe from their trips abroad. The essentials of the Quaker penal philosophy differed somewhat from British thinking, mainly in the stress on individual rehabilitation that would occur through solitary imprisonment coupled with religious instruction, hard work in the cell, and prison visitation.[12] Like the British, these reformers were also concerned with matters of health, internal security, and deterrence of crime.

After the Revolution, the Walnut Street Jail, itself a distinct improvement over earlier Philadelphia prisons, was operating in a manner that scandalized Philadelphia reformers. A thriving bar was maintained by the warden, who sold liquor at inflated prices. Prisoners, as in many of the English prisons visited by Howard, sometimes obtained money to buy alcohol by selling their clothes or forcing new prisoners to give up some of their possessions. All classes of prisoners, male and female, mingled freely; allegedly women had themselves arrested and confined for fictitious debts in order to consort with the male prisoners, and generally riotous and disorderly behavior prevailed throughout the institution.[13] Although some prisoners were held in irons, escapes were common. Inmates were sometimes kept after their legal release date, had so-called garnish fees levied upon entering, and occasionally were denied access to local clergy. In 1787 a grand jury found that "the gaol has become a desirable place for the more wicked and polluted of both sexes."[14]

In 1790 the Walnut Street Jail, founded as a city and county prison, became a state penitentiary. That same year legislation promoted by the Prison Society called for the construction of a small cellblock within the prison enclosure to provide solitary confinement for the "more hardened and atrocious offenders," who were now being given prison terms rather than death sentences.[15]

This Penitentiary House clearly reflected elements of design mentioned by John Howard: two floors of cells raised on arches above ground level, each with eight cells facing a corridor that, as in most English and Irish jails of the time, had a dividing wall down the center to prevent communication between inmates on opposite sides.[16] The cells were six by eight by nine feet high and vaulted in brick. Double cell doors, one of wood and one of iron, led to the corridor. A small window, high on the exterior cell wall, was covered by a double iron grating and had exterior louvers to prevent the inmate from looking down on the street. There was neither a bed nor a bench, merely a

William Birch (1755–1834), *Jail in Walnut Street, Philadelphia*, 1800. Engraving, 8⅛ x 10⅝". The Library Company of Philadelphia.

mattress. Each cell had a water tap and privy pipe, and heat was supplied by stoves in the passageways.[17] The inmate was allowed to read in his cell at some stage of his imprisonment and to see the turnkey or guard once a day but was never to be outside his cell, even in the passageway. Following his visit to the Walnut Street Jail, the French philanthropist Duc F.-A.-F. de la Rochefoucauld-Liancourt wrote: "In this situation, separated from every other individual, given up to solitude, to self-reflexion, and to remorse, he can communicate only with himself."[18]

The Penitentiary House was supposed to demonstrate the philanthropist-reformers' evolving strategy for treating criminals, but the evidence suggests that the cells were used primarily for the punishment of those who committed prison infractions rather than for offenders specifically sentenced by the courts to solitary confinement.[19] With the rapid population growth of Philadelphia and the eastern part of the state, the Walnut Street Jail soon became overcrowded, and complaints of bad associations, idleness, and poor supervision were aired once more. Members of the Prison Society, viewing the situation at the Walnut Street Jail, were convinced that in spite of the small-scale isolation cellblock built there, the prison would never be able to prove the value of the system of separate confinement. To accomplish that an entirely new prison on a grander scale was needed.

II CRUCIBLE OF GOOD INTENTIONS

Plan of the Walnut Street Jail in 1798, showing the addition of the Penitentiary House (marked *D*) and workshops around a central court behind the existing building. From *The Philadelphia Monthly Magazine*, vol. 1, 1798.

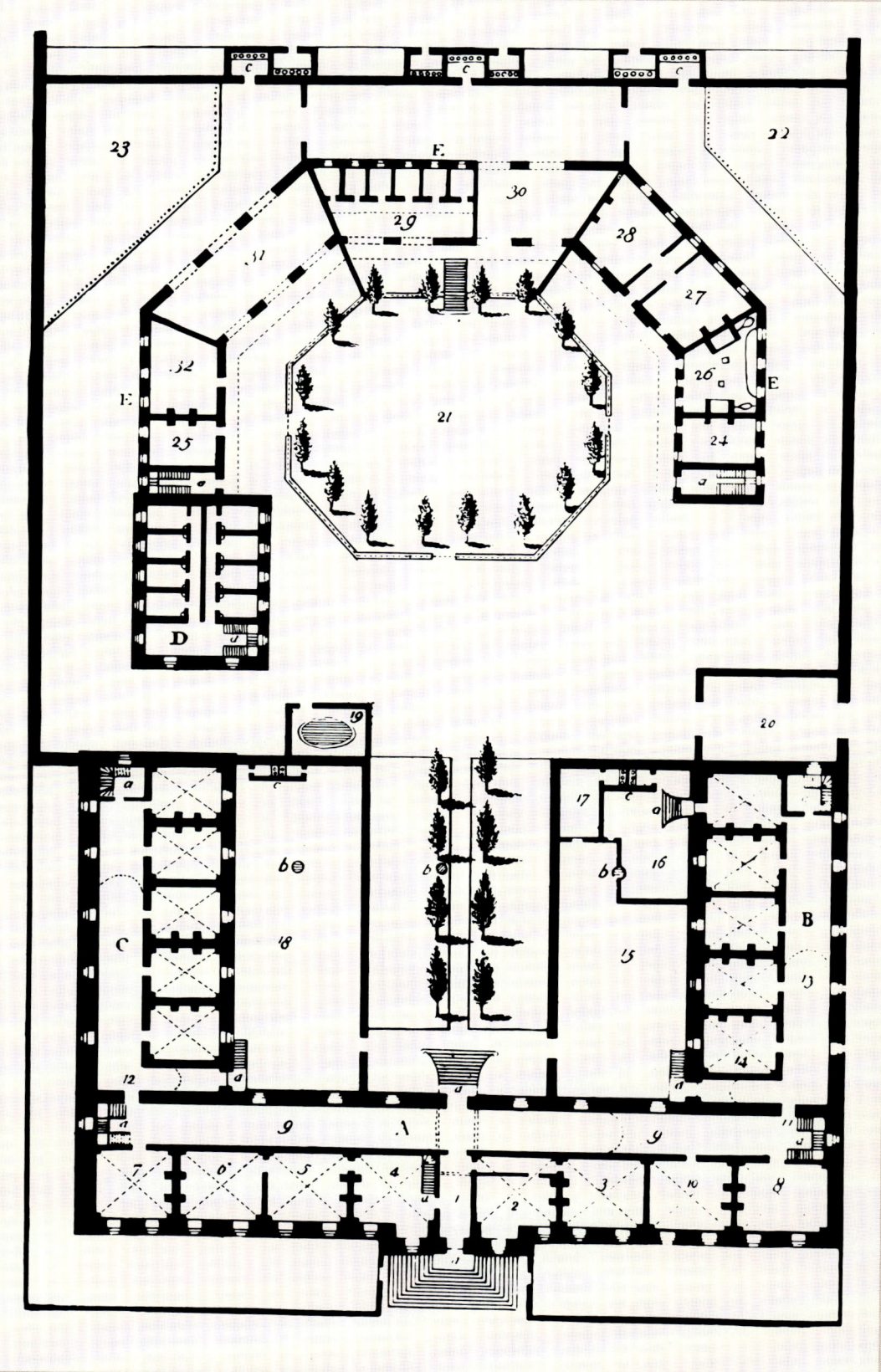

Curiously, in view of Pennsylvania's long identification with the system of separate and solitary confinement, the first serious test of isolation in cells in the United States was in New York State. Under the pressure of overcrowding in the state penitentiary at Greenwich, a new prison at Auburn was opened in 1816 with the customary congregate housing. In response to developments in Philadelphia, however, a few years later a new wing was built with individual cells to try solitary confinement. The experiment lasted from 1821 until 1823, when it was discontinued as a complete failure. The tiny cells at Auburn (three feet eight inches by seven feet six inches) had inadequate ventilation, heat, and plumbing. Because no regimen of activity had been developed before the system was put into use, many prisoners suffered from mental illness and poor health. Subsequently, New York and other states abandoned absolute confinement in cells for a modified system that combined day work outside the cells in congregate workshops under a rule of complete silence, and nighttime confinement in small, individual sleeping rooms.

During the first two decades of the nineteenth century, discussions among the Philadelphia reformers resulted in an increasingly detailed rationale for separate and solitary confinement as the only proper method for treating criminals. On a mission to the United States to study American prisons, the French representatives Gustave de Beaumont and Alexis de Tocqueville captured that rationale in their report *On the Penitentiary System in the United States, and Its Application in France*:

Thrown into solitude . . . [the prisoner] reflects. Placed alone, in view of his crime, he learns to hate it; and if his soul be not yet surfeited with crime, and thus have lost all taste for any thing better, it is in solitude, where remorse will come to assail him.

And further:

Can there be a combination more powerful for reformation than that of a prison which hands over the prisoner to all the trials of solitude, leads him through reflection to remorse, through religion to hope; makes him industrious by the burden of idleness, and which, whilst it inflicts the torment of solitude, makes him find a charm in the converse of pious men, whom otherwise he would have seen with indifference, and heard without pleasure?[20]

While there was general agreement in the Prison Society about the value of separate confinement, debate as to whether the prisoners should be allowed to work continued. One group held that solitude becomes more effective without employment because the offender is compelled to reflect, and they opposed labor "except the study of the holy scriptures, connected with affectionate religious instruction."[21] Since, they reasoned, the guilty mind makes every effort to avoid reflection, and activity drowns out conscience, the prohibition of labor would mean that corrective results could be achieved in a shorter period of time.

But another group, equally influential, emphasized that labor had an intrinsic curative and moral value, and that it was necessary to preserve the health and sanity of the inmates and teach them habits of industry, as well as to defray some of the expenses incurred by their imprisonment. Reformers were uneasy with the thought of idle lawbreakers supported by hardworking, honest citizens, regardless of the theoretical justification for reflective inactivity. On April 23, 1829, this point of view prevailed, when an act of the legislature to reform the penal laws of the Commonwealth stipulated that labor would be mandated for sentences of solitary imprisonment in Pennsylvania.[22]

Meanwhile, repeated lobbying by the Prison Society and the board of the Walnut Street Jail resulted in the state legislature authorizing the construction of the Western Penitentiary at Pittsburgh in 1818 and the Eastern State Penitentiary near Philadelphia in 1821.[23] The Pittsburgh prison opened in 1826. Flawed by its inadequate heating, improper ventilation, and lack of sanitary facilities in the cells, it was a complete failure, torn down seven years after it opened. The legislative acts authorizing the two new prisons had made no mention of prisoners working, and the Pittsburgh prison had provided solitary confinement without labor. The controversy over prison labor was still unresolved when Eastern State Penitentiary was planned, and no legislative decision had yet been made about the issue even when the first cellblocks were being built. But the individual cells in the new prison were of sufficient size to allow compliance with the 1829 law mandating inmate labor that passed the same year the prison opened. All the elements were in place, and the great experiment could begin.

III

Building the Ideal Prison

NORMAN JOHNSTON

John Neagle, (1796–1865), *Portrait of John Haviland*. Oil on canvas, 33 x 26". The Metropolitan Museum of Art, New York. Alfred N. Punnett Fund, 1938.

The arena in which the new ideas would be tested, Eastern State Penitentiary, was to be located not more than two and a half miles from the State House and was to have a capacity of 250 prisoners. The authorizing legislation passed on March 20, 1821, stipulated that the prison was to be built on the plan of the Western Penitentiary, then under construction near Pittsburgh, and provided for an initial appropriation of $100,000; additional financing was to come from the proceeds of the sale of county lots. Eleven Building Commissioners were appointed by the governor and authorized to purchase a site, select plans, and superintend construction. The Building Commissioners were free to modify the project as long as they observed the principle of solitary confinement.[1] This group first met in April 1821, and included outstanding Quakers and other leading Philadelphia citizens, among them Samuel R. Wood, the first warden of the penitentiary. Joining them later that year was philanthropist Roberts Vaux, who was to become one of the strongest forces guiding the new prison.

Twenty-three sites for the prison were initially considered, both on the west side of the Schuylkill River and east of the river on plots scattered from Race Street north to what is now Fairmount Avenue. An elevated piece of farmland just north of the city limits in the Fairmount section was chosen and purchased for $11,500. The owners were allowed to remove any property from the lot, including an orchard of cherry trees. Because of the orchard, Eastern State Penitentiary was commonly known, even abroad, as Cherry Hill.

In May 1821 architects were invited by the Building Commissioners to submit designs. A prison in which inmates would be kept in solitary confinement for their entire sentence made unprecedented demands on the design of the cell itself, where the prisoner would sleep, eat, receive religious instruction, and perhaps work. Each cell required plumbing and an individual exercise yard. To correct the

III CRUCIBLE OF GOOD INTENTIONS

Albert Newsam (1808–1864) after Henry Inman (1801–1846), *Portrait of Roberts Vaux*, c.1845. Lithograph by P. S. Duval and Co., 13⅝ x 10¼". The Library Company of Philadelphia.

persistent problems of earlier prisons, the plan had to allow close surveillance not only of inmates in their cells and yards, but also of the guards. In the words of the Building Commissioners:

Good design is to produce, by means of sufferings principally acting on the mind and accompanied with moral and religious instruction, a disposition to virtuous conduct, the only sure preventive of crime; and where this beneficial effect does not follow, to impress so great a dread and terror, as to deter the offender from the commission of crime in the state where the system of solitary confinement exists.[2]

Reacting to conditions prevalent in American and European prisons, the commissioners were resolved that the new penitentiary would provide a healthy environment. Since current theories of contagion and disease assigned an important role to "miasmas," or foul air, the siting of the prison and the internal arrangement of buildings had to be carefully planned to provide the best ventilation. At the same time, given the dismal record of most prisons to achieve their essential function—to keep their occupants confined—the structure had to be designed to prevent escapes.

When the call for designs went out, the issue of inmate labor was still unresolved; as far as can be determined, no mention was made of prisoners working in their cells in the public announcement of the competition for the prison design.

Choosing an Architect

Of four proposals submitted, only two were given serious consideration: one by newly arrived British architect John Haviland (1792–1852) and the other by William Strickland (1788–1854), a well-known local architect and the designer of the Western Penitentiary near Pittsburgh. Strickland submitted a circular, or "panoptic," plan, apparently close to that of the Western Penitentiary.[3] Haviland's was a so-called radial, or hub-and-spoke, plan, similar to many county prisons then being built throughout Britain.[4]

At first, when submissions for the design were opened in July 1821, Strickland had a clear advantage over the younger and less experienced Haviland; only one commissioner preferred Haviland's design. Later, changes in the membership of the commission resulted in nearly equal numbers supporting Haviland and Strickland. Parliamentary maneuvering and frequently acrimonious charges and countercharges characterized meetings for an entire year. At the request of the commissioners, both architects submitted new, modified plans and estimates, particularly reworking details of the front building. Haviland's preliminary design, although featuring a relatively plain facade, had called for a larger prison than Strickland's. Haviland added towers and gothic details to his revised design, which Strickland's supporters characterized as "more fitted in its external shew and internal convenience for the dwelling of a nabob than the keeper of the prison."[5]

Although the commissioners had not yet approved a plan, they appointed Strickland supervising architect in the fall of 1821. The commissioners still opposed Strickland's plan for an octagonal wall and circular cellblock, and they let contracts for building a rectangular perimeter wall. In the meantime, Strickland left for Europe, returning in February 1822 to begin superintending construction of the wall. In March, Strickland's design for a front building was approved, but on May 14 the commissioners reversed themselves and approved Haviland's design for a larger front building instead. A week later Haviland's entire plan was approved, and the decision was ratified by the governor. The commissioners finally preferred Haviland's radial plan to Strickland's circular design because it would be cheaper to build and less expensive to supervise once in operation. Also, the supervising engineer for Strickland's Pittsburgh prison had expressed his dissatisfaction with its circular plan and a preference for radial schemes.[6] Strickland reluctantly agreed to supervise the building of the prison according to his rival's designs, but in a letter to the commissioners he stated that he could not assume responsibility for the success or final cost of the project.[7]

In September 1822, after bitter argument among the commissioners, Strickland was relieved of his duties, and later the same month, Haviland was appointed supervising architect. It is not known how much construction Strickland actually oversaw, but it could not have been much.

Haviland and His Plan

Haviland was born on December 15, 1792, near Taunton in Somerset, England. At nineteen he was apprenticed to the London architect James Elmes (1782–1862). Elmes had designed several prisons and in 1817 published a small pamphlet on prison planning that revealed a careful reading of John Howard's works and a general enthusiasm for prison reform that he may have passed on to his pupil. In 1815, when barely finished with his apprenticeship, Haviland traveled to Russia; his aunt had married Count Morduinoff, a minister of the imperial government, who invited the young architect to St. Petersburg. Haviland hoped to secure an appointment in the Corps of Engineers, but the job did not materialize. During his visit he met Philadelphia-born Gen. Sir George von Sonntag, then an admiral in the Imperial Navy. Perhaps under his influence, and armed with letters of introduction from both von Sonntag and John Quincy Adams, then United States Minister to Britain and formerly to St. Petersburg, to influential people in the United States including President James Monroe, Haviland moved to Philadelphia to practice architecture.[8]

Once there, Haviland established an "architectural drawing academy" at Seventh and Chestnut Streets with fellow Briton Hugh Bridport. In 1818 he published the first of three volumes of *The Builder's Assistant*, the first American publication to illustrate the correct Greek orders, then fashionable in British architectural circles. Haviland and Strickland vied for the design of the Second Bank of the United States and for the first Western Penitentiary. Strickland won both competitions. Haviland's early important commissions were the

John Neagle, *Portrait of William Strickland*, 1829. Oil on canvas, 30 x 25". Yale University Art Gallery, New Haven. Mabel Brady Garvan Collection.

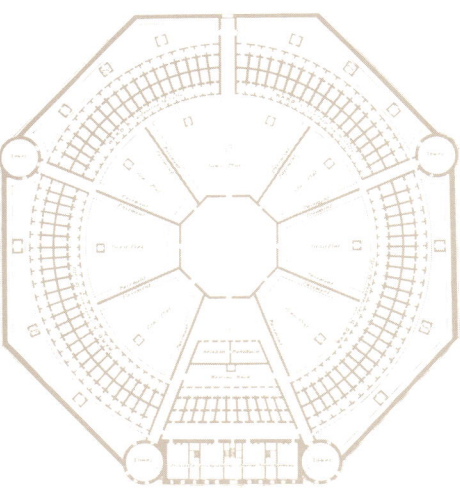

Plan of the Western Penitentiary, near Pittsburgh, by William Strickland, opened in 1826 and razed in less than seven years. From *Report of William Crawford, Esq., on the Penitentiaries of the United States* (London: Parliamentary Papers, 1835).

III CRUCIBLE OF GOOD INTENTIONS

First Presbyterian Church at Seventh and Washington Streets and St. Andrew's Episcopal Church at Eighth near Spruce Street, now St. George's Greek Orthodox Cathedral.

As Eastern State Penitentiary was being constructed, Haviland rapidly achieved both national and international prominence, receiving commissions for a variety of buildings. In Philadelphia he designed the Franklin Institute (now the Atwater Kent Museum); the Philadelphia Arcade; the Pennsylvania Institution for the Deaf and Dumb (now the University of the Arts); dwellings on Chestnut Street; and alterations to the Walnut Street Theatre. Near Norfolk he built the United States Naval Asylum. During this same period he designed the second Western Penitentiary, replacing Strickland's ill-starred project; the Rhode Island Penitentiary; the first Missouri Penitentiary; the Essex County courthouse and jail, in New Jersey; and the famous Halls of Justice and jail in New York City, known as the Tombs. For most of these projects, the architect was also the builder—a practice common at the time and one that explains his involvement with so many buildings over relatively long periods. With all this activity he still had time to help found the American Institution of Architects, to bring out two more volumes of *The Builder's Assistant*, and to revise Owen Biddle's *Young Carpenter's Assistant*.

Haviland eventually designed twelve state or county prisons.[9] He also submitted plans for a penitentiary in Quebec and sent drawings to British, French, and Russian officials in the hope of receiving commissions. None resulted from these efforts, despite the fact that by the end of the 1830s Haviland had acquired a reputation as the world's foremost prison architect. The county prison at Lancaster, Pennsylvania, completed in 1851 and in use until the 1960s, was his last prison project. He died on March 28, 1852, and was buried in the crypt of St. Andrew's Church.

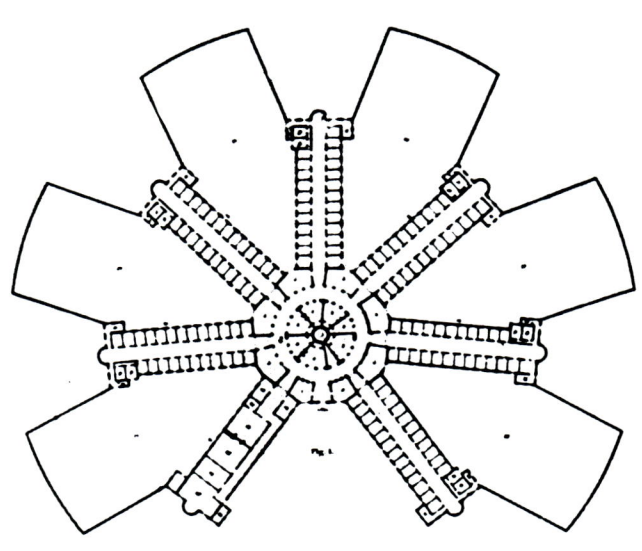

Plan for the proposed London Lunatic Asylum, by James Bevans, 1814. Engraving. Private Collection.

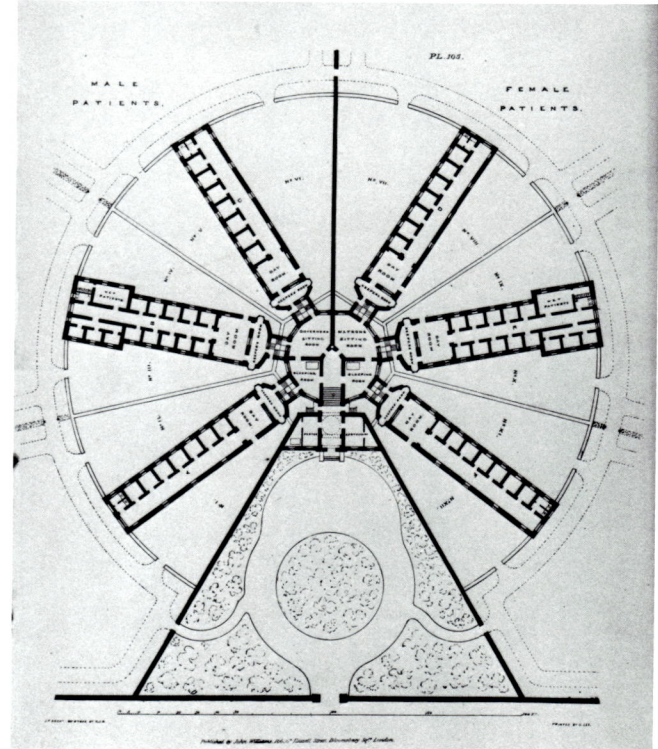

Plan of the Cornwall Lunatic Asylum, Bodmin, England, by John Foulston, erected in 1818. Engraving. From John Foulston, *The Public Buildings Erected in the West of England* (London: J. Williams, 1838).

Building the Ideal Prison

Draft of Haviland's description of his design for Eastern State Penitentiary, 1821. John Haviland, daybook no. 1. Haviland Papers, Van Pelt Library, University of Pennsylvania.

While engaged on the Eastern State Penitentiary project, Haviland found himself in the middle of a dynamic group of prison reformers, and soon identified himself completely with the emergent Pennsylvania system and its controversies; in a letter of 1842, he referred to himself as the "Original Architect of the System."[10] He had personal contact with members of prison societies in various states, as well as with the representatives of foreign governments, who flocked to Philadelphia to view his prison, and he corresponded with many reformers around the world. Among his papers, a partial list of books apparently from his personal library suggests a wide acquaintance with prison-reform literature of the period.

Writing to the commissioners in 1821, Haviland remarked that he had selected the hub-and-spoke form for the prison to promote "*watching, convenience, economy* and *ventilation*."[11] He did not indicate the sources of his inspiration, but they lie in a variety of plans for prisons and asylums built beginning in the 1780s in England and Ireland. These complexes consisted of cell wings radiating in a semi- or full-circle array from a center house, where the governor or warden lived; they were usually on a small scale, and the surveillance of inmates and guards was often poor.[12] Some of these institutions, which Haviland undoubtedly knew, bear a close resemblance to his early ideas for the Philadelphia prison. For example, a plan was published in 1814 for a proposed London Lunatic Asylum, designed by James Bevans. It had seven single-story wings radiating from a central hub. The center building contained service facilities and a circular passageway, called an inspection gallery. Bevans's hospital was never built, but the proposal was published when Haviland was studying in London, and may have provided inspiration for his ideas.

A similar structure on a smaller scale was built near Bodmin, Cornwall, in 1818. This county asylum, designed by John Foulston, consisted of a central hub and six radiating two-story wings with patients' rooms and dayrooms. Some provision was made for observation of the wings from the governor's and matron's quarters in the center, and the keepers' rooms in each wing, but given the number of partitions, surveillance could not have been very good.[13]

Haviland's original plan and specifications for Cherry Hill are lost, but must have been similar to an idealized version published in 1830.[14] This consisted of an octagonal center connected by corridors to seven radiating single-story cellblocks, each containing two ranges of large single cells with individual exercise yards. In his daybook Haviland described the original concept for the center of the building as follows:

Crucible of Good Intentions

The circular Building in the center of this Plan, contains a range of twenty six cells, with their yards, and other conveniences constructed similar to the before described cells, this number of cells being under the same roof as the wash-house and Laundry would be a very appropriate situation for the confinement of the Female Prisoners. The Kitchen, Bakehouse, Breadroom, Wash-house, Laundry and Store rooms; are conveniently adjoining each other, of sufficient capacity for their respective purposes, with ample light from windows inserted over the roofs of the circular cells.[15]

He suggested that a chapel or a cistern for water storage could be located on the floor above. "Eight strong dungeons" were to be located on the basement level of this center building, each connected with the floor above by a separate staircase, and although these cells would be unlighted, they were to have individual fireplaces. An observation tower was to top the structure.

The Uses of Style

The early years of the nineteenth century have been characterized by one historian as "the fancy dress ball of architecture . . . in full swing."[16] The recent explorations of Egyptian, Greek, Roman, and medieval sites had provided architects with a vast new repertory. Haviland's teacher, James Elmes, was fond of the Greek orders, and Haviland illustrated them himself in his early books and used them on some of his buildings. For the facade of Eastern State Penitentiary, however, he chose a restrained gothic similar to some of the jails that had been erected in England in the decades before he left for America.[17] The front building, or "keepers' house," was, in the architect's words, to be in the "Anglo Norman" style, complete with castellated towers and a portcullis and flanked by walls with blank windows and guard towers at each front corner. Although the expense of his towers and the massive front building was criticized, he continued to use the gothic style for most of his subsequent prisons.[18]

Prisons in the nineteenth century were not intended solely to be places to punish and reform wrongdoers; they were also tangible symbols calculated to remind free citizens what might befall them should they break the law. The exterior design, therefore, had a psychological as well as a physical function: to deter the potential criminal. To fulfill this grave responsibility, the facade had to convey the austerity, the sorrow, and the grimness of the regimen within if it were to be "appropriate," and present such a forbidding and awesome appearance to passers-by that they would be disinclined to engage in any actions likely to land them inside. Haviland's teacher had commented on the powerful effect of London's newly rebuilt and infamous Newgate prison:

Without doubt the most appropriate and correct design in the metropolis, or perhaps in Europe; for, no one viewing this edifice can possibly mistake it for any thing but a gaol, the openings as small as convenient, and the whole external aspect made as gloomy and melancholy as possible.[19]

The Building Commissioners of the Philadelphia prison went on record as saying:

The exterior of a solitary prison should exhibit as much as possible great strength and convey to the mind a cheerless blank indicative of the misery which awaits the unhappy being who enters within its walls.[20]

The architect had to balance his artistic ambition with the critics' concern that an elaborate facade, no matter how fortresslike, would be expensive and seem luxurious to the poor.[21] A British commentator observed that "a prison should always be a prison," suggesting:

The gaol ought never to divest itself of the character of a place of severe yet not unnatural probation and expiation; a place inspiring a wholesome dread, and to get into which the lower orders shall feel it most undesirable. But . . . the sumptuous externals now becoming so general in this country, are little calculated to create and foster this salutary fear. How should they? . . . Is it not well known that the repulsive appearance of our workhouses does more to keep the poor from applying for admission than the mere restraints and regulations within? . . . The unrealized ideas of the penal institution—the ponderous gates, the lofty walls, the sombre character of the entire building, these were and are, where they exist, undoubtedly elements of repression; they leave a good deal to the imagination, but at the same time they furnish it with a positive suggestion of much tangible cause of terror.[22]

Initial Construction

In reading both U.S. and foreign descriptions of Eastern State Penitentiary from the 1820s, one is often struck by the discrepancies in the accounts concerning the details and dimensions of the cells and cellblocks, the way spaces in the front building were used, and even the dates when buildings were begun and completed. But the fact is that details of the design changed with the construction of each new cellblock. Haviland was a relatively inexperienced architect working on what was at the time the largest public structure in the country. Few prisons of this size had been attempted anywhere; the architect was learning with each year of building and with each wing of cells, especially as portions of the prison began to be occupied. No one had ever tried to design quarters for twenty-four-hour occupancy of large numbers of inmates for their entire term of imprisonment. Central heating of large-scale buildings and the use of indoor plumbing were at their most rudimentary beginnings. No architect had yet begun to solve these mechanical problems adequately, even on a small scale.

After John Haviland (1792–1852), *Bird's Eye View of the New State Penitentiary, Now Erecting Near Philadelphia*, 1824. Engraving by C. G. Childs, 18¾ x 27⅜". Free Library of Philadelphia. A view of Eastern State Penitentiary with the proposed seven symmetrical single-story wings as in Haviland's preliminary proposal.

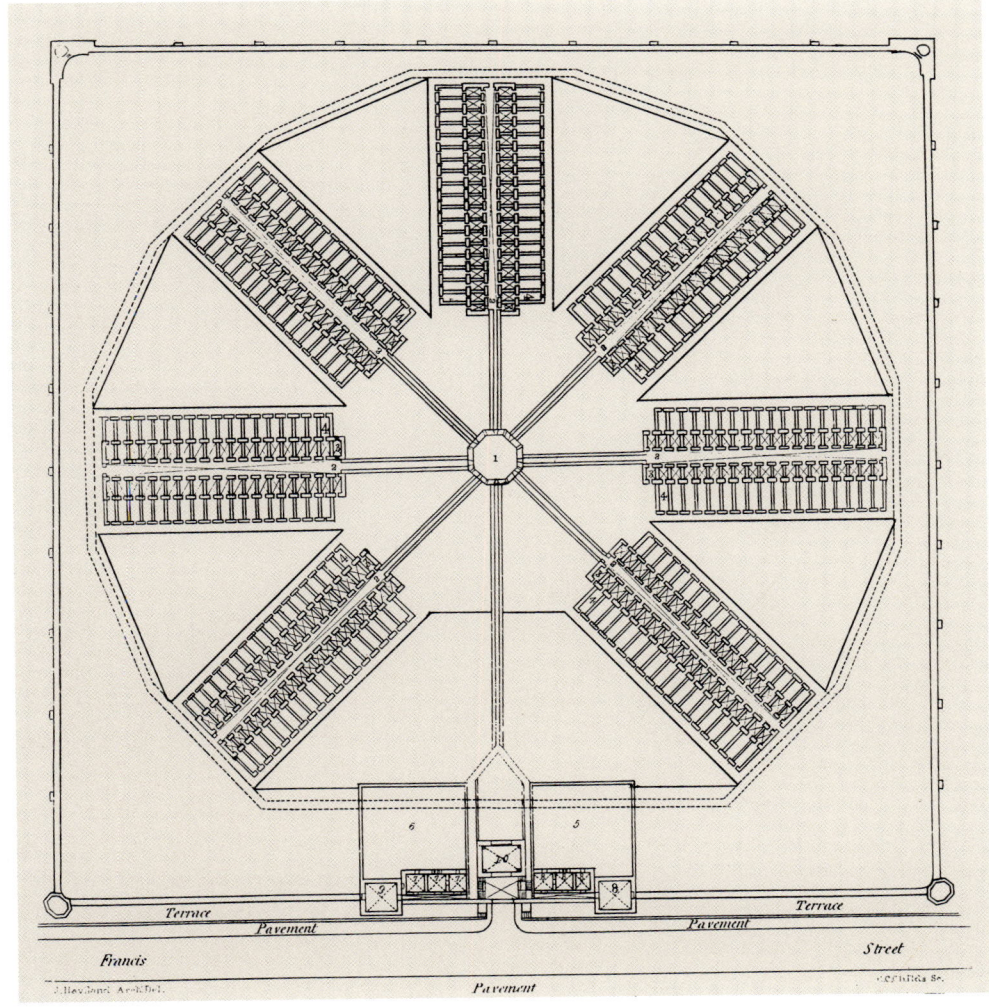

After John Haviland, *Plan of the Eastern Penitentiary*, c. 1829. Engraving by C. G. Childs, 8 1/16 x 5⅛". From George W. Smith, *A View and Description of the Eastern Penitentiary of Pennsylvania* (Philadelphia: C. G. Childs, 1830). An idealized version of Haviland's symmetrical plan for Eastern State Penitentiary.

Robert Newell (active 1856–1903), *Entrance to Eastern State Penitentiary*, c. 1870. Albumen print. 9¼ x 7⅞". The Library Company of Philadelphia.

George Lehman (died 1870), *Eastern Penitentiary of Pennsylvania Near Philadelphia*, 1833. Lithograph by Childs and Inman, 9 1/16 x 12". The Library Company of Philadelphia. Built on the site of a cherry orchard, Eastern State Penitentiary was known as Cherry Hill.

The perimeter wall and the foundation for the front building were constructed first. Work was in progress by May 1822. The cornerstone was laid on May 22, 1823. In it were placed plans and elevations and a metal plate with the inscription:

Penitentiary, For the Eastern District of the State of Pennsylvania. Founded Agreeably to an Act of Assembly passed on the 20th day of March, in the year of our Lord one thousand eight hundred and twenty-one.[23]

The front building, two hundred feet long, has a square tower at each end and, to enhance security, a single entrance in the center. The original entrance was an impressive, arched gateway twenty-seven feet high, with an iron portcullis and two massive doors of oak studded with iron rivets, surmounted by a bell tower eighty feet high. An ugly modern entrance was added to the old one in 1938, disfiguring the front of the prison as it was built in the 1820s.[24]

Entering the prison one came into a vestibule arched by a brick vault stuccoed to look like stone. There was a balcony on the third-floor level on three sides that probably connected the right and left wings of the front structure. Beyond this vestibule, one had to pass through two sets of iron gates, only one of which would be opened at a time.

III CRUCIBLE OF GOOD INTENTIONS

Original feeding aperture for an individual cell in block three at Eastern State Penitentiary. Photograph, 1975.

The east (right) side of the front building housed the warden's apartment. The second level on the opposite side contained keepers' quarters and offices. One of the large tower rooms was a meeting place for the Prison Inspectors, the governing body of the penitentiary once it was in operation. Originally the top floor on the west end of the building was an infirmary with a separate staircase. A room on this level under the central tower was reserved for the apothecary. Initially, some of the upper rooms were also used to house female prisoners. On the ground floor, accessible only by stairs leading to the yards at the rear of each wing of the building, were a kitchen, a bakery, and offices. The walled yard behind the warden's quarters was his garden; the yard on the opposite side contained some small buildings for the processing of new prisoners.

On its completion, the central octagonal building differed greatly from Haviland's first designs. The proposed service facilities and dungeons were eliminated and the center became an observation point, clear of all partitions, with a view into each of the seven corridors. On the second level were water tanks and an open platform that allowed the guards a view of the prison yard, the walls, parts of the individual exercise yards, and portions of the roofs of the single-story cellblocks.

As inmates were to serve their entire sentence in their cells, these were very generously proportioned by nineteenth-century and even late-twentieth-century standards. The thirty-eight cells in block one, the first constructed, were eight by twelve feet and had brick vaults ten feet high at the crown. An iron latticework door and a solid wooden door connected each cell to an individual exercise yard the same width as the cell and eighteen feet long. Initially there were no doors from the corridor to the individual cells; access to the cell was only through the outside iron door in the wall of each inmate's exercise yard. There were, however, rectangular openings in the corridor wall through which food and work materials could be passed. There was also a small peephole so guards could observe the prisoner without being seen. The cell was lit by a small skylight in the arched vault. As first designed, the bed was suspended on chains so it could be swung against the wall during the daytime. A tap for fresh water and vents for fresh air and heating were also provided in each cell.

To minimize the opportunities for communication between inmates, Haviland decided against the customary toilet buckets and instead designed a rudimentary flush toilet for each cell, with individual soil pipes leading directly to a central sewer located under the corridors. Water from a reservoir was flushed through the pipes periodically. Haviland hoped this arrangement would prevent the sending of messages between adjacent cells. Nevertheless, inmates were often able to make contact with each other, and the design of the toilets and their flushing system had to be changed several times to prevent prisoners from tapping out messages through the empty pipes.

By 1829 the front building, the central rotunda, and the first of three cellblocks were largely completed. There still had been no legislative agreement on whether prisoners should work or not, either in their cells or communally. This was finally clarified on April 23, 1829, when an act to reform the penal laws specified that prisoners should "suffer punishment *by separate or solitary confinement at labour . . . in the cells or work yards.*"[25]

While workmen were still coming into the unfinished prison it received its first prisoner in October 1829. Blocks two and three were occupied in 1831. It had by this time become obvious that the prison as planned, with seven single-story wings of thirty-eight cells, would soon be woefully inadequate for the increasing number of inmates. The original plan for 250 cells clearly had to be modified. Haviland was forced to redesign the four blocks that remained to be built to accommodate two stories; in 1831 work was begun on the

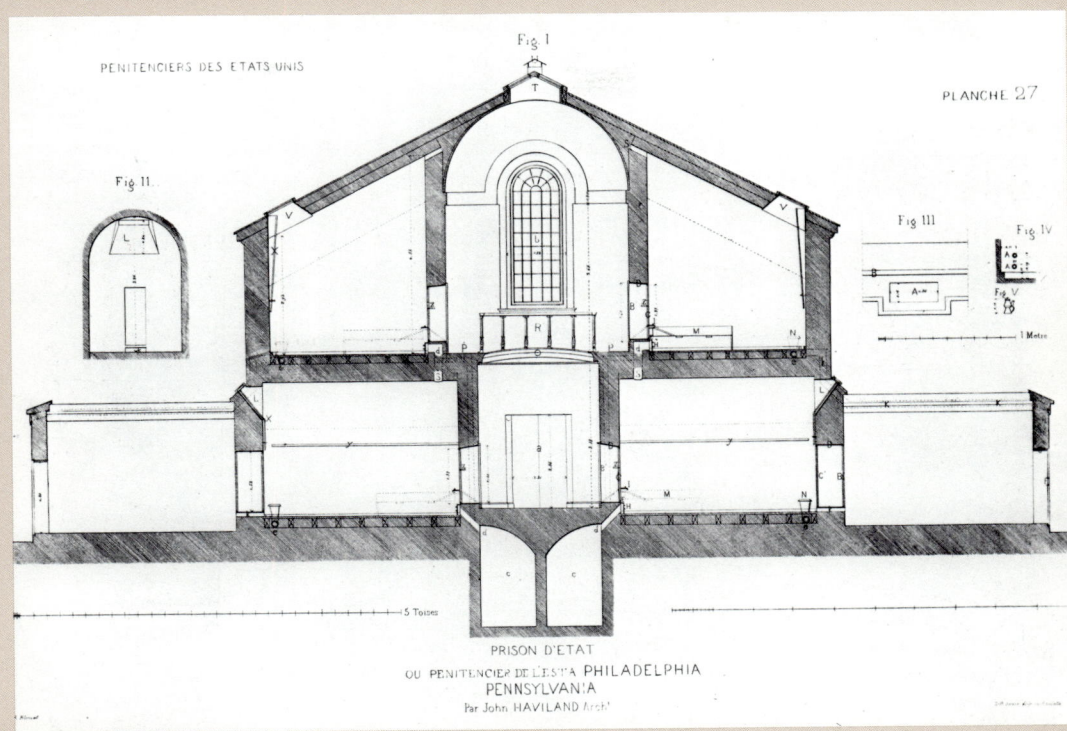

Cross section of a two-story cellblock at Eastern State Penitentiary, 1837. Engraving. From Frédéric-Auguste Demetz and Guillaume-Abel Blouet, *Rapports sur les pénitenciers des Etats-Unis* (Paris: Imprimerie royale, 1837).

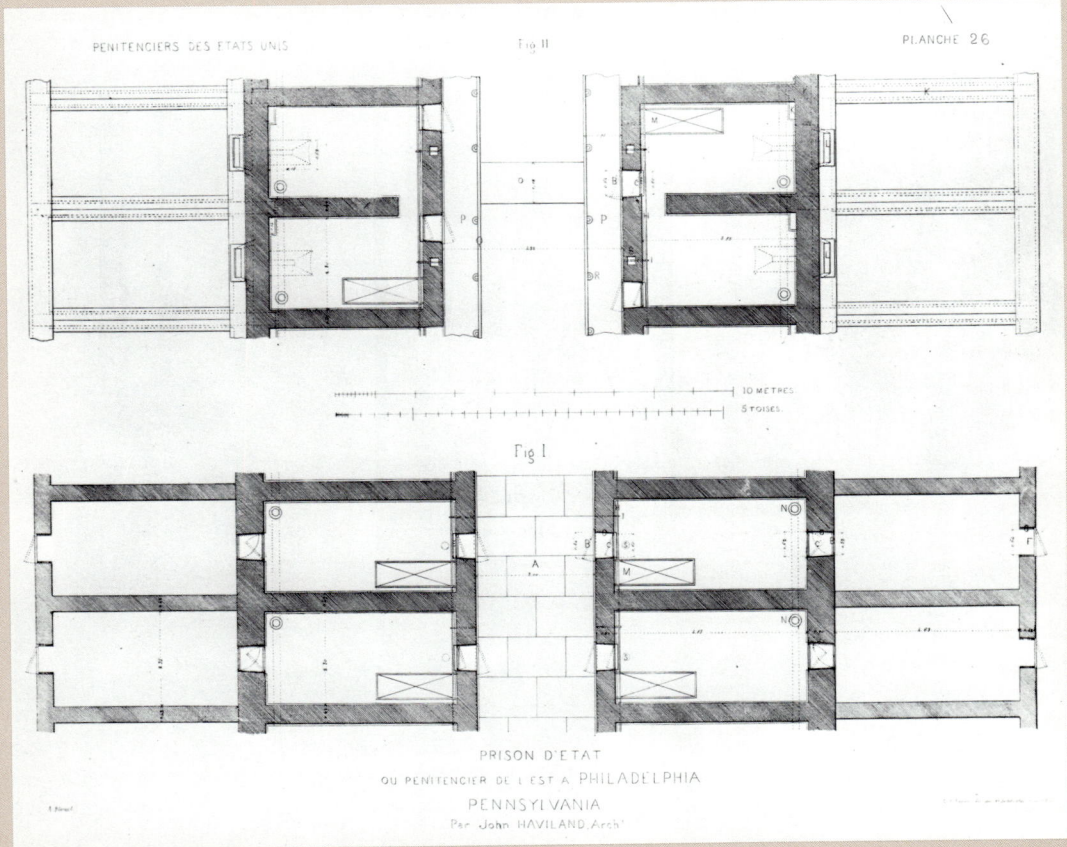

Plan of the first- and second-story cells at Eastern State Penitentiary, 1837. Engraving. From Demetz and Blouet, 1837.

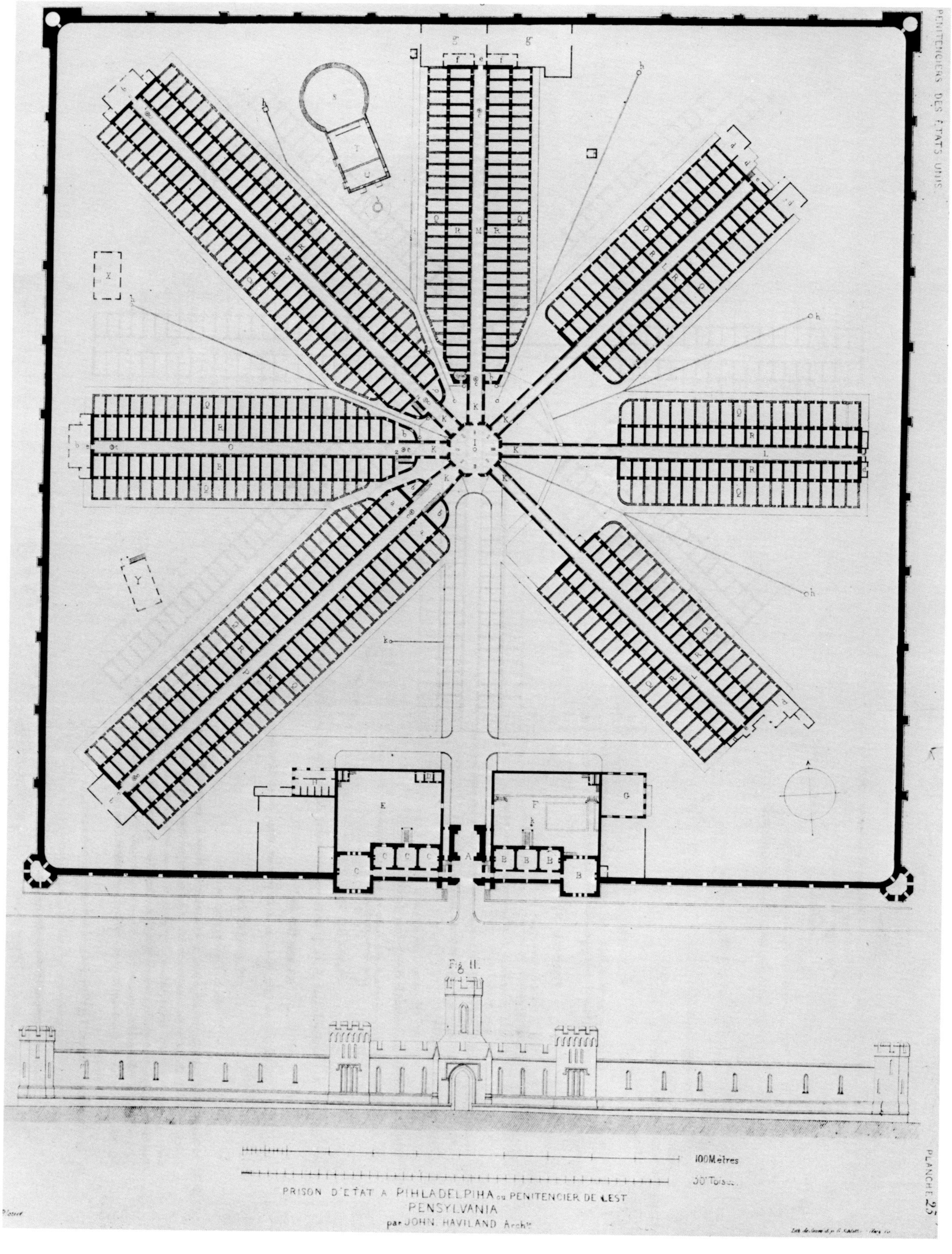

III Crucible of Good Intentions

Cost estimate for the perimeter wall of Eastern State Penitentiary, probably from 1822. John Haviland, daybook no. 1. Haviland Papers, Van Pelt Library, University of Pennsylvania.

Plan of Eastern State Penitentiary, 1837, showing Haviland's design as completed in the previous year. Engraving. From Demetz and Blouet, 1837.

foundations for blocks four, five, and six. The architect now faced the problem of providing exercise areas on the second floor. This was solved temporarily by providing a door between two adjacent cells, which were of somewhat smaller dimensions than the first-floor cells. One room was to be used for exercise and work space, the other for sleeping.

As access to cells in the first three blocks by way of the exterior yard had proved inconvenient, cells in subsequent blocks had doorways on the corridor, each fitted with a solid oak door with a peephole and an inner iron latticework door with a small opening through which to pass food. The earlier cellblocks were refitted with similar doors connecting each cell to the corridor. The stone floors in the cells were too cold in the winter, so wooden floors were laid in all the cells. In 1834 the last of Haviland's proposed seven wings was begun, and by 1836 the prison was completed. It could then house about 450 prisoners in solitary confinement, compared to the 250 for which it was originally planned.[26]

Problems Arise

By far the most complex problems Haviland encountered were those of heating, ventilation, and plumbing. Not only were large-scale applications of such systems yet to be perfected, but the mechanical means available permitted inmates to communicate with their fellows.[27] Haviland first placed stoves in the tunnels under the cellblock corridors. Small flues in the floors and walls were to allow hot air to rise into each cell and to release stale air from the building. The system did not work, and a number of inmates became ill from carbon-monoxide fumes. In the end, the architect adopted an English system using high-pressure hot water, with pipes looping into each cell then out into the corridor before turning into the adjacent cell, so that inmates tapping out messages would be detected by the guards. By all accounts this heating system was barely adequate in the winter but was undoubtedly superior to most central-heating systems of the time.[28]

Ventilation was a major problem. The walls of the exercise yards blocked air circulation, the small skylights rarely provided sunshine or fresh air, and the inadequate flues contributed to the continual dampness of the cells. An author writing in 1853 quoted from the penitentiary physician's report of 1848 describing the bedding and clothing made wet by the humidity in the cells:

The importance of fresh pure air to the well-being of both mind and body, need not in these days be insisted upon; yet it must be acknowledged, that the ventilation in the Eastern Penitentiary is defective. It is true, when the doors communicating with the yards and corridors are open, a stream of fresh air rushes through the cells, which imparts life and vigour to their inmates; but when these are closed—and this, under present arrangements, must average more than twenty-two hours a day—the current almost ceases, and a more or less vitiated atmosphere alone remains to be inhaled by the prisoners.[29]

Providing an adequate water supply and toilet facilities also required ongoing design changes. The customary routines of congregate prisons, such as lining up for wash basins and water or cleaning and emptying toilet buckets, could not be followed. Each cell required a basin and a cold-water tap. Initially the water supply was located in tanks on the second level of the central building, the water being provided by the Fairmount Waterworks. When the two-story cellblocks were erected it became necessary to build a reservoir in the prison yard, sink a well, and provide a steam engine for pumping, as the municipal water pressure was inadequate to supply the upper floor. Each cell also had a toilet, a cast-iron cone attached to a waste pipe. When the stoves initially were located in

III Crucible of Good Intentions

the underground tunnels, which acted as large heating ducts, they warmed the contents of the sewer pipes, increasing the already noxious odors present in the cells. The prison physician observed that the clothes of a person merely walking through the corridors would be impregnated with these odors.[30]

Aside from the usual technical problems that accompany a large construction project, there were other crises, such as that of ensuring the workers' sobriety during their hours of employment. A daily ration of spirits was provided to the workmen, but it was felt necessary to discourage further drinking during the workday. Although the commissioners opposed the opening of bars in the area, one was established across from the construction site on Fairmount Avenue. The commissioners passed new rules stating that anyone subject to intoxication would be fired.

Although accusations of graft and favoritism were sometimes leveled by critics during this period, the only serious financial scandal associated with the construction of the prison was the curious loss of $1,000 in building funds, a not inconsiderable sum at the time, by the president of the Building Commissioners, Peter Miercken.[31]

Critics and Supporters

Even before the penitentiary was finished in 1836, it had become both famous and controversial, not only in the United States but also in other countries. New York State, after renouncing its poorly thought-out, brief experiment with separate confinement in inadequate prison buildings, became, along with Massachusetts, an aggressive proponent of an alternative method of prison treatment: the so-called Auburn system. In this system prisoners slept in tiny cells at night and worked in complete silence in communal workshops during the day. For decades the partisans of the Pennsylvania and the Auburn systems were at odds, trading accusations of cruelty and citing increased costs to taxpayers and high rates of mental illness among prisoners. Not only did supporters of the two systems attack one another's prisons in publications and conferences in the United States, but the controversy also extended to international meetings and public dialogues abroad, especially in Europe. Ultimately the collective pride of Philadelphians and Pennsylvanians became entangled with the rightness of the system developed at Cherry Hill, just as reformers in Massachusetts and New York saw the reputations of their states identified with the effectiveness of their rival system. In such a climate, reports, books, and claims often hid as much as they revealed. Countless publications accumulated, arguing the merits or drawbacks of each method of penal treatment. Criticism of the Philadelphia prison generally centered on four issues: the cost; the possibly adverse effects on the physical and mental health of the inmates; the comparative cruelty of the system; and the degree to which it actually resulted in reform.

The extravagance and size of the front building initially drew the most criticism. It was pointed out that inmates themselves could not see the elaborate facade. In their 1833 report covering the two rival U.S. prison systems, Gustave de Beaumont and Alexis de Tocqueville characterized the construction of Cherry Hill as having incurred enormous unnecessary expenses: "The greater part had no other object than the ornament of the edifice."[32]

The first appropriation from the Pennsylvania legislature barely covered the cost of the construction of the perimeter wall and front building. Not only did Haviland stubbornly adhere to his conception of a grand facade and gothic details, but his desire for high-quality construction guided his specifications for the entire prison. At one point auditors questioned the need for thirteen fancy marble fireplace mantels in the front building. Haviland offered personally to pay the difference between those already installed and the price of more utilitarian substitutes. The original appropriation for the prison had been $100,000; by 1834, before it was finished, nearly $800,000 had been expended, and only 311 cells had been constructed. For a number of reasons it is difficult to establish the exact cost per cell, but it was clearly many times that of other prisons built at the time.[33]

But the criticism did not stop when expenditures for the new building came to an end. Questions were raised almost immediately about both the physical and mental health of the inmates. Miasmic theories of contagion led many to consider whether the dampness, the lack of fresh air, and the emanations from toilets in the cells caused rates of illness higher than usual in other prisons.[34] Loyal supporters of the system sometimes admitted that there were a few health problems, but they also presented their own statistics to disprove the critics' claims.

The mental health of the prisoners was a contentious issue. The annual reports of the prison physician carefully recorded all cases, including their remission or cures. In the pamphlet war that raged between the New York and Massachusetts reformers and the Philadelphia faction during the 1830s and 1840s, authors traded "insanity" statistics. The lack of any reliable figures for the general population, however, and the fact that people suffering from mental illness would often come through the criminal justice system to enter the prison makes reliable evaluation of the conflicting claims difficult.

There were a few critics, such as Charles Dickens, who found the system of isolation to be inherently cruel. This argument was parried by the defenders of the Pennsylvania system, who emphasized the cruelty of the corporal punishment used to maintain order at prisons such as Sing Sing and Auburn in New York State.

Did all of this effort and expense result in reform? Over this issue as well

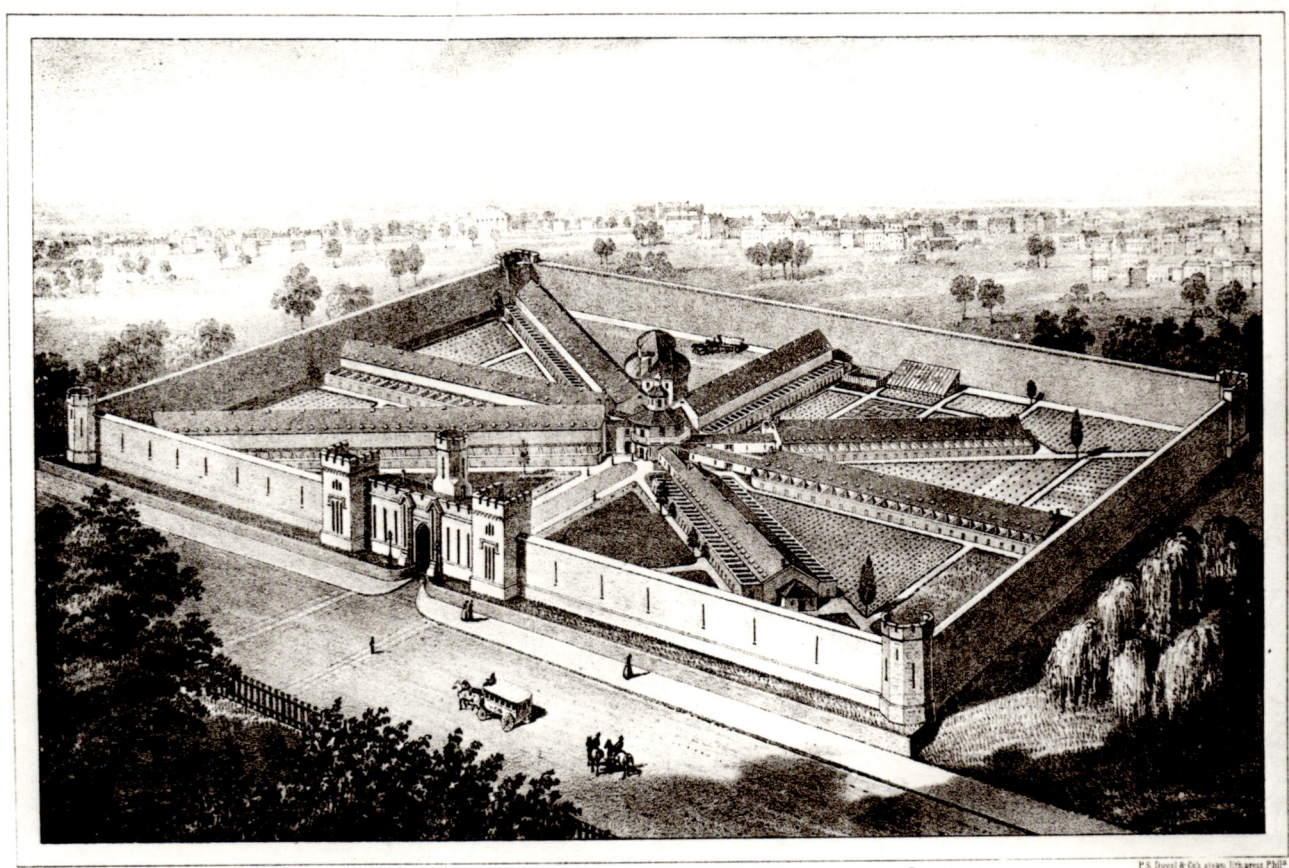

Samuel Cowperthwaite, convict number 2954, *The State Penitentiary, for the Eastern District of Pennsylvania*, 1855. Lithograph by P. S. Duval and Co., 8¾ x 10⁷⁄₁₆". The Library Company of Philadelphia. The three cellblocks to the right are shorter than they appear in this view.

the two camps traded arguments, statistics, and anecdotal evidence of lifelong scoundrels dramatically rehabilitated under one system or the other. The Philadelphia reformers, however, perhaps to justify the higher cost of building and running their prison, stressed its reformative capabilities more than did those espousing the Auburn system.

Although some critics found the cost of the prison inappropriate and even scandalous, the Building Commissioners and the Philadelphia establishment were ultimately won over. Their confidence grew as emissaries, tourists, and philanthropists from around the world came to view the progress of the prison and its revolutionary system. In these early months of operation the managers and supporters of the new prison confidently and vigorously brushed aside most criticisms, making alterations to the physical structure and the internal regimen as they launched the first large-scale application of an idealistic and radical new penology. The great experiment in the modification of criminal behavior had begun. All of Europe and most of the American states and Canada were watching.

IV
Noble Ideas Collide with Reality

NORMAN JOHNSTON

Cellblock nine corridor at Eastern State Penitentiary, 1890s, with food carts. From Michael J. Cassidy, *Warden Cassidy on Prisons and Convicts* (Philadelphia: Patterson and White, 1897).

A British prison administrator once likened a prison to "a monastery inhabited by men who do not choose to be monks."[1] Eastern State Penitentiary was intended by its creators to operate in many ways like a monastery, and most certainly the prisoners were there unwillingly. The first prisoners were overseen by Warden Samuel Wood, a former member of the Building Commissioners, an inspector of the Walnut Street Jail, and a steadfast Quaker. As warden he was required to live on the premises, having his quarters in the eastern portion of the front building. He was not to be absent for a night without written permission from two members of the Board of Inspectors. During the first years of the prison at least six families besides the warden's lived within the walls, either in quarters in the front building, in the towers, or in a house remaining on the grounds of the yet-unfinished facility.

The warden was responsible to the Board of Inspectors, which met regularly and made nominal visits to the prison. Board members were public-spirited citizens, usually prominent in business or politics, like Anthony Drexel, a banker. Roberts Vaux, whose son would later become warden, was on the board for fifty-three years, all but ten of them as president.

In 1829 prisoners were already being received while parts of the prison were still under construction, and entering prisoners came in the front gate along with hundreds of workmen, building materials, staff, and tradesmen. Prisoners were to be sent to Eastern State Penitentiary from counties in the eastern judicial districts of the state, but the counties were often reluctant to do so inasmuch as they had to bear a portion of the cost of incarceration. Because the federal government had no penitentiary system during most of the nineteenth century, convicted federal felons were also sometimes sent to Cherry Hill. Although during the 1830s and 1840s men and women would be jailed for up to twenty-one years for

IV CRUCIBLE OF GOOD INTENTIONS

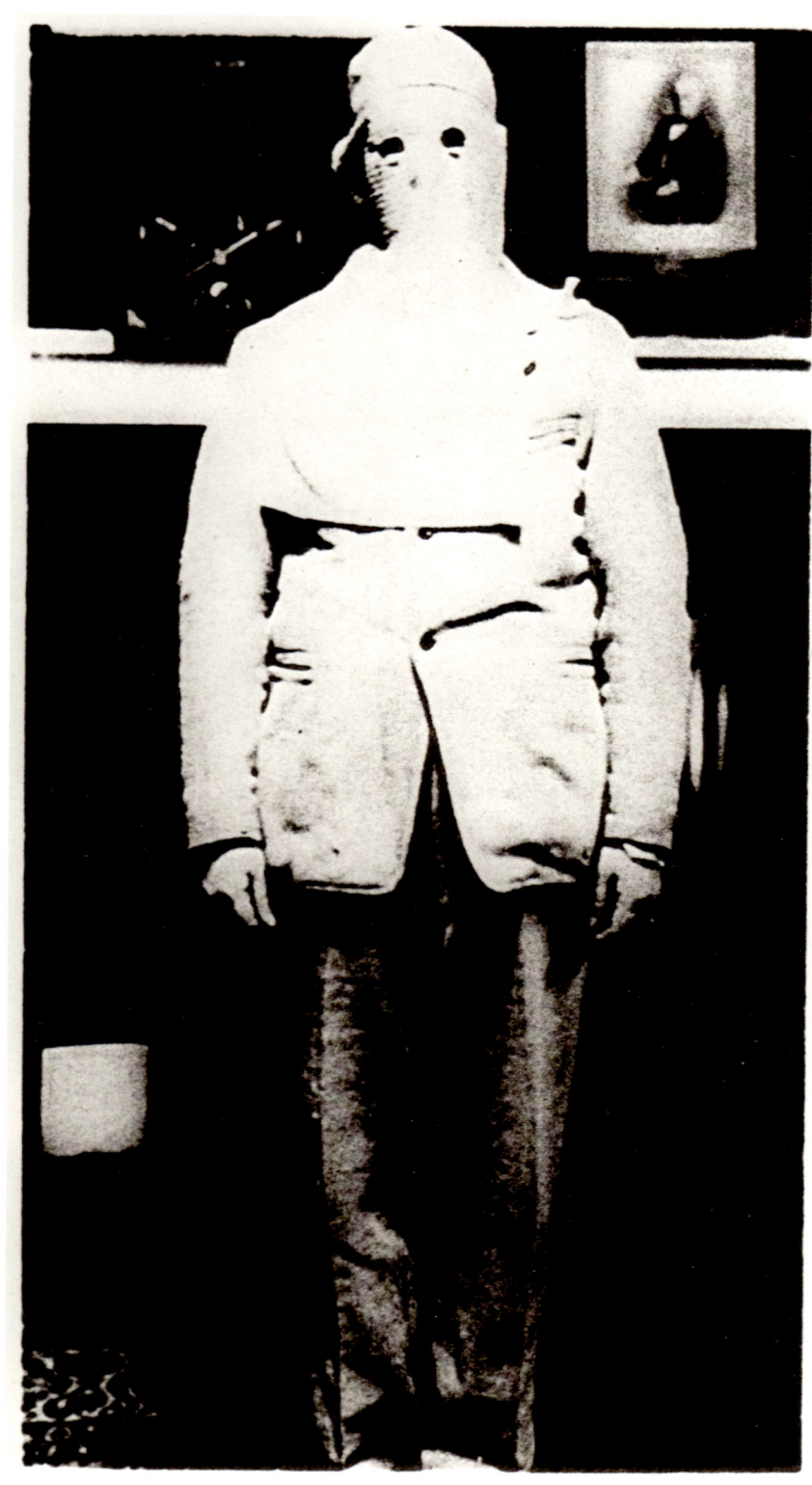

Masked prisoner in Eastern State Penitentiary, late nineteenth century.

murder or a second offense of kidnapping, most of the sentences were much shorter. Average sentences were still brief in 1870, when two and a half years was usual. When the prison opened in 1829, the most common offenses were larceny, burglary of houses or businesses, and horse theft.

In the first four years of operation, 153 white males, 52 African American males, and 4 African American females were admitted to Cherry Hill. Female prisoners were probably initially kept in one of the upper-level tower rooms in the front building but were later transferred to the second level of block seven. In 1852 they were moved to cells in one of the original one-story blocks, probably block two. During the nineteenth century pregnant prisoners delivered their babies in the prison. Female prisoners continued to be housed in the penitentiary until 1923, when they were transferred to the State Industrial Home for Women at Muncy, the first state prison in Pennsylvania built specifically for women. As there were no separate prisons in the state for younger offenders, occasionally boys were sent to Cherry Hill, perhaps for their entire sentence. A boy of twelve from Bucks County, committed for arson, was among the early inmates.

Admission Procedures

On arrival, prisoners were examined by the physician. Inmates relinquished their clothing and belongings, which were stored until their discharge. They were given baths and their hair was closely cropped. In the winter each would be issued a pair of woolen trousers, a close-fitting jacket, a shirt, two handkerchiefs, two pairs of "yarn stockings," and a pair of "coarse leather" shoes. Cotton trousers would be issued in warmer weather. Admission procedures were stipulated in the 1829 act reforming penal laws:

He or she shall then be examined by the clerk and the warden, in the presence of as many of the overseers as can conveniently attend, in order to their becoming acquainted with his or her person and countenance, and his or her name, height, apparent and alleged age, place of nativity, trade, complexion, colour of hair and eyes, and length of his or her feet, to be accurately measured, shall be entered in a book provided for that purpose, together with such other natural or accidental marks, or peculiarity of feature or appearance, as may serve to identify him or her, and if the convict can write, his or her signature shall be written under the said description of his or her person.[2]

Each prisoner received a number that corresponded to his or her place in the order of admissions: number 306 was the 306th prisoner to be committed since prisoner number 1 on October 25, 1829. Henceforth the inmate was known by that number; it was hung over the cell door and sewn on clothing.

A hood was then placed over the prisoner's head to prevent his gaining "topographical knowledge" of the prison layout or catching a glimpse of another inmate, and he was led through the prison yard to a cell, where the hood was removed and the rules of the institution were explained.[3]

The Cells

The cells at Cherry Hill were unusually large by contemporary and even today's standards, ranging from seven and a half by twelve feet to seven and a half by sixteen feet. The exercise yards were eight feet wide and eighteen feet long, with twelve-foot-high walls. Spartan furnishings were provided by the prison: an iron bedstead, a clothes rack, a stool, a tin cup, a food pan, a spoon, knife, and fork, a water can, a brush for cleaning, a fine-tooth comb, a "wash-hand basin" and a clean towel, supplied weekly. A workbench, loom, or other equipment would sometimes be provided in the cell. Next to the wall was a cast-iron funnel-shaped hopper, which served as a toilet. Above this was a cold-water tap. The walls were whitewashed. These furnishings varied little during the nineteenth century.

By the 1880s the beds consisted of boards on two wooden trestles and straw-filled ticks and blankets. When the occupants of the cells changed, new straw mattresses were supplied.

During his first days in the cell, the new prisoner would not be given work or reading materials. He would have to make a request for either, and a Bible and inspirational reading material would be given to him as "a favour." A whale-oil lamp would normally be provided until 9 o'clock. The inmate could usually open a skylight in his cell to get some air. In warm weather the wooden door to the exercise yard could be left open; after the earlier cellblocks were fitted with wooden doors to the corridor, these, too, could be opened slightly for cross-ventilation.

The prisoner now began a regimen of nearly complete solitude, a routine intended to prevent the corruption that thrived in prisons where mingling was permitted. To maintain their anonymity, male prisoners would be addressed by their numbers, seldom by name. If for some unusual reason it became necessary to take an inmate from his cell, he had to don a mask. Violation of the rules prohibiting communication or unnecessary noise, such as singing or whistling, could result in the denial of dinner, the main meal of the day, for a week. Guards wore socks over their shoes and the wheels of the carts that brought food to the cells were covered with leather to ensure silence in which the prisoners' attempts to communicate could be overheard. Visitors sometimes commented on the unearthly silence inside the prison.

Inmates arose at daybreak, or, in the summer, between 4:30 and 5:00 a.m. Breakfast was served at 7 o'clock, dinner at 12 noon, and supper at 6 o'clock. Prisoners were to be in bed by 9 or 10 o'clock. If they were skilled laborers, they might be permitted to work in their cells after dark. Weather permitting, they were allowed out in their individual exercise yards for an hour a day, except on Sundays. Inmates in adjacent cells went out in different shifts so they could not converse over the walls.

Although the inmate was never to communicate with his fellow prisoners, have visits from family or friends, see a newspaper, or hear from any source about events in the outside world—not even the name of the president of the United States—he or she was allowed contact with a limited number of people. Each of the overseers was expected to meet daily with a specified number of prisoners assigned to him, usually about forty. The overseers provided instruction in trades, brought meals, and gave advice. At night, watchmen maintained order. Inmates might also have occasional contact with the warden, the prison physician, and other staff. They were visited periodically by members of the local clergy and the Prison Society.

The Separate System in Practice

The defining characteristic of the new prison, and the one most difficult to achieve in practice, was the isolation of inmates from one another. Keeping the inmates separated for their entire sentence from other prisoners they would never see, let alone get to recognize, as they ate, worked, and exercised in their own spaces appeared to be a simple task. It was not. Furthermore it is clear that right from the start the prison violated its own rules: inmates were used for various housekeeping tasks around the prison and, without their masks and prison garb, served at dinner parties given by the warden.

The first investigation of Cherry Hill in 1834–35, carried out by a joint legislative committee, revealed that female prisoners were working in the kitchen, a practice that continued until the late nineteenth century, and on at least one occasion female inmates were seen being returned to their cells intoxicated, having sampled the contents of the warden's liquor cabinet while on assignment. The investigative committee also reported that a prisoner was observed sitting next to a guard in the central rotunda, reading a newspaper.[4]

IV CRUCIBLE OF GOOD INTENTIONS

Other incidents recorded by Prison Society visitors or officials indicate that prisoners moved about, assisting with routine maintenance or working with the free laborers. Prisoners helped to complete the construction of the prison in the 1830s, and inmates were primarily responsible for building the new cellblocks begun in 1877 as part of a major expansion. Prisoners were probably routinely assigned janitorial tasks. The annual report of 1850 noted the death of a prisoner who had been exposed constantly to wet floors while mopping cellblock corridors.

One early authority noted that two men were sometimes placed together in a cell so that one could learn a trade from the other;[5] a visitor from the Prison Society recorded in 1853 that two German-speaking prisoners were placed in the same cell so that the newcomer, who did not understand English, could be instructed in shoemaking. The first investigation disclosed also that prisoners were occasionally put in cells with others who needed watching over for medical reasons. In the 1880s the inmates who worked in the piggery, the greenhouse, and the flower garden were selected supposedly because they were unlikely to be harmed by association or, in other cases, were physically or mentally "weak" and therefore beyond the danger of contamination. Prisoners who were regarded as insane might also have the conditions of separate confinement relaxed.

Although a mask was to be worn any time the inmate left the cell, it is difficult to imagine that in the activities described in the reports, prisoners complied with the rule. In 1855 the warden noted in his journal: "The new order of the Board requiring the yard and shop men, in passing from and returning to their cells, to wear hood-caps, with eye holes, was put into practice this morning."[6] This suggests that before then the rule had lapsed. In 1887 the prison physician set up a gymnasium in which six convicts at a time were permitted to exercise with their masks on, and in 1892 masks were still being used to bring men for their baths. It was not until October 1903 that wearing masks around the prison was discontinued, except when requested by the prisoner; masks were no longer issued to new arrivals.

In spite of precautions, inmates were able to communicate with one another from time to time, even if they were not among the few assigned to work outside their cells. Some prisoners communicated through the walls or empty sewer pipes using a "rapping alphabet," a technique common in prisons all over the world.[7] Prison administrators were also aware that prisoners threw notes weighted with pebbles over the walls separating the exercise yards, making contact even with prisoners two cells away. Officers on the balcony of the central building could not see into all of the individual exercise yards, and during periods when prisoners were outside, guards sometimes walked around the exterior of the range of attached yards to detect any efforts at communication between inmates. The investigation of 1834–35 revealed that an inmate in his yard could converse with the occupant of the cell directly above through the second-floor ventilation flue. Prisoners in some cells were also able to communicate with neighbors through the skylights if they stood on a workbench or stool, so the skylights were nailed shut in 1852. In 1831 one ambitious prisoner was able to make a hole in the wall of his cell to make contact with his neighboring inmate.

The wooden cell doors to the corridors were opened on Sundays for religious services and left ajar on hot days for ventilation. These doors were probably not opened wide enough for the inmates to see each other, but given the length of the cellblocks and the inability of the few guards to keep track of every occupant, it is likely that prisoners out of earshot of the overseer were able to talk, exchanging names and biographical information in just the way reformers were trying to prevent. In fact, visitors from the Prison Society noted in 1845 that on Sundays, when a smaller complement of keepers was on duty, the cellblocks were very noisy. Dr. Robert Given, the prison physician in the early decades of operation, nevertheless wrote that estimates of communication among the prisoners were exaggerated, and that if prisoners were in contact, it did not average more than ten minutes a day.[8]

The facts concerning surreptitious communication between prisoners could easily be kept from the public and critics. What was not so easily concealed, to the embarrassment of the proponents of the system, was the increased crowding in the prison, which forced the greatest deviation from the ideal of separate confinement. As early as March 1841, the Prison Society visiting committee reported with disapproval that some cells contained two male convicts. By 1867 there were 569 inmates in 540 cells, and by 1876, prior to a major building program, there were only 585 cells for 795 inmates: over half the prisoners in a penitentiary organized on the separate system thus shared cells.

Between 1877 and 1894 four new cellblocks without exercise yards were constructed, but by 1897 there were 1,200 prisoners in only 765 cells. While Cherry Hill officials continued to tout the Pennsylvania system in public, they gradually substituted the term "individual treatment" for "separate system." Before the turn of the century the prison's population approached 1,400, with as many as four inmates occupying one cell.

The picture of the sparsely furnished cell and the bare exercise enclosure was as misleading as the usual impression of solitary confinement. Some prisoners had small gardens in their yards for vegetables, flowers, or fruit grown from seeds provided by Philadelphia merchants. In the winter some of these plants were brought into the cells. Some prisoners were allowed to keep small pets, such as birds and rabbits. When Charles Dickens visited Cherry

Noble Ideas Collide with Reality

Cell interior at Eastern State Penitentiary, mid-nineteenth century. From Richard Vaux, *Brief Sketch of the Origin and History of the State Penitentiary* (Philadelphia: McLaughlin Brothers, 1872). The prisoner's food was passed through the aperture in the iron lattice-work door.

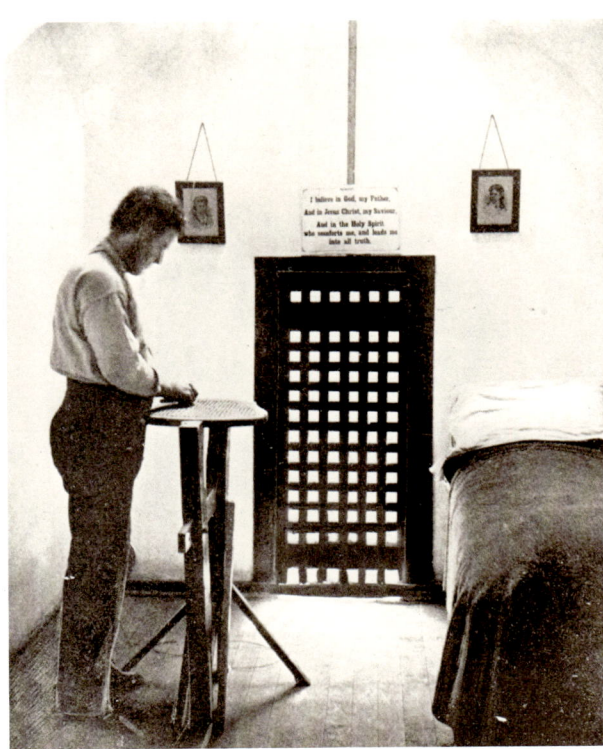

Cell interior at Eastern State Penitentiary, mid-nineteenth century, showing the exercise-yard door. From Vaux, 1872. The prisoner is caning a chair seat.

Hill in 1842, one inmate was interviewed in the corridor rather than in his cell, which smelled too strongly of pets. Inmates were sometimes permitted to decorate the walls of their cells and engage in hobbies, although no materials officially were provided for this. Dickens described the cell of a German inmate sentenced to five years for larceny:

With colours procured . . . he had painted every inch of the walls and ceiling quite beautifully. He had laid out the few feet of ground, behind, with exquisite neatness, and had made a little bed in the centre, that looked by the bye like a grave. The taste and ingenuity he had displayed in everything were most extraordinary.[9]

Dickens also described a female prisoner's "snow-white room" hung with the work of a former occupant.

In most prisons the inmates were strictly prohibited from keeping pets, decorating their cells, or accumulating homelike possessions, and it would appear that during the nineteenth century the regimen at Cherry Hill was milder than it was acknowledged to be. It is not clear if this resulted from humane gestures on the part of guards showing favoritism toward some prisoners or if it represented official policy.

The ways an inmate was allowed to alter his cell with the tacit approval of the officers should be distinguished from surreptitious modifications and possession of contraband. Undoubtedly, as prisoners were permitted more freedom of movement within the prison toward the close of the century, a greater variety of illicit goods and services became available to them. In 1885 a Philadelphia newspaper article describing life at Cherry Hill mentioned prisoners cooking meals on improvised stoves and hooking up a homemade telephone system between cells.[10]

Diet

Meals for the prisoners were prepared in the kitchen and bakery, initially located

IV Crucible of Good Intentions

in the basement of the front building, and subsequently in rooms at the ends of some cellblocks, until a separate kitchen was built later in the nineteenth century. The food was brought to the cells on three wagons nicknamed "Washington," "Franklin," and "Lafayette" by an inmate waiter.[11] Food carts on the second level of some of the cellblocks ran on rails.

Breakfast usually consisted of a pint of coffee, cocoa, or green tea, although the Prison Society visiting committee reported a beverage of hot water and milk and a mix of bread and Indian mush (corn meal) served as the first meal. Dinner, served at midday, was the primary meal. It consisted of either ¾ pound of boiled beef "without bone" or ½ pound of pork, a pint of soup, and an unlimited helping of potatoes or boiled rice. Supper consisted of a plentiful supply of Indian mush sweetened with a small amount of molasses, and sometimes sauerkraut made of turnips or cabbage, with tea as the beverage. Salt was provided on request and vinegar "as a favor." Generally a pound of wheat or rye bread a day was divided among the three meals. In 1848 the Prison Society visiting committee found that the inmates were getting "very good" food but being served only two meals a day. The diet slowly changed: by 1852 tea was being sweetened with sugar, and dinner usually consisted of beef or mutton, with beef at least twice a week and Indian meal pudding once a week.

By the end of the century, inmates were still being served meals in their cells, although the menu was more varied:

Sunday	*meat pie with onions and potatoes*
Monday	*soup of beef, potatoes, onions, turnips, cabbage, peas, and rice*
Tuesday	*bologna, pickles, shortcake*
Wednesday	*same as Monday*
Thursday	*bean soup with beef*
Friday	*stew of beef, potatoes, onions, herbs, and flour*
Saturday	*same as Monday*[12]

Roast beef and potatoes were served every twenty-five days. Prisoners might supplement their fare with lettuce, tomatoes, grapes, and even peaches and plums they cultivated in their exercise yards. Prisoners were not required to finish their meals when served, but if mess kits were not clean by the next meal, food was withheld. When family visits were finally permitted, no food was allowed to be brought into the prison under any circumstances.

The diet at Cherry Hill should be seen in relation to American cuisine and particularly working-class eating habits in the nineteenth century. All foreign visitors were impressed by the amount of meat Americans ate. Although industrialization and urbanization meant poorer nutritional levels for workers and an actual decrease in average height, at mid-century food was relatively plentiful.[13] Even so, while fresh meat was available, salt pork, for example, was preferred over fresh pork. A mix of salt pork and corn was eaten three times a day by many families. City wage-earners ate few perishable luxuries, and fresh meat perhaps once a week. Vegetables were not popular. Besides potatoes and cabbage, one vegetable a day might be served—turnips or other preservable vegetables in the winter and fresh produce during the growing season.

Religious Instruction and Education

Although religion figured strongly in the thinking of those who sought to reform criminals through the use of solitary confinement, it is telling that the 1821

A cell without an exercise yard at Eastern State Penitentiary, as designed and built under Warden Cassidy between 1877 and 1894. Engraving. Location unknown.

James Earle McClees (1821–1887), *Eastern State Penitentiary, Philadelphia*, c. 1858. Albumen print, 10 x 13". The Library Company of Philadelphia.

enabling legislation for Eastern State Penitentiary stipulated that the chaplain was to be unpaid. Initially no suitable minister could be found to donate his services, but, by 1831, clergymen were visiting the prison as part-time volunteers. It was more effective to set up makeshift chapels in each cellblock than to have clergy attempt to meet with each convict in his or her cell. On Sundays seven Protestant clergymen preached from the ends of each block from 9 to 10 o'clock. The wooden doors of the cells were left ajar during the service, with a curtain strung up along the middle of the corridor to prevent prisoners in opposite cells from seeing one another. Two officers with socks on their shoes patrolled the corridors to detect conversations.

In 1838 a "moral instructor," or chaplain, was appointed by the Board of Inspectors and paid from public funds. Visits to prisoners in their cells were to take place at least once a month, although Prison Society officials found in the 1840s that some inmates saw the chaplain less often and sometimes were neglected altogether. Some community members objected to the appointment of an official chaplain, fearing that it would lead to sectarian proselytizing. To counter this risk, Catholic priests, rabbis, and ministers of different Protestant denominations were invited to visit the prison. Prisoners were not taken outside their cells for church services until 1914. In the mid-nineteenth century they were allowed to have religious newspapers.

Officials visiting from abroad were generally favorably disposed to the Cherry Hill system, but the lack of religious services in the early days and the absence of a chapel, a prominent feature of all new nineteenth-century European prisons, were seen as puzzling inconsistencies.

Until 1854, when a full-time teacher was hired, the moral instructor at Cherry Hill was also in charge of the library. Records of the Pennsylvania Prison Society indicate frequent allocations of funds for the purchase of books, particularly religious tracts. The warden and the moral instructor determined which books were appropriate for the prisoners to read; in the 1830s the warden ordered the removal of a pamphlet containing orations and a brief biography of Thomas

Paine, describing him as promoting "deistical doctrines."[14] By the 1880s inmates who could read were given a printed catalogue of library books, a slate, and chalk. They were to write the call numbers of up to fifty books or magazines on the list. The librarian would then select one or more of the available books or, if none of the inmate's selections was on the shelves, substitute another suitable work. Many books were religious; others were uplifting fiction. The catalogue of this period suggests that the average inmate may have found some of the volumes tough going: Pope's translation of *The Iliad*, Byron's *Childe Harold's Pilgrimage*, Sir Walter Scott's *Chronicles of the Canongate*, and issues of the *Atlantic Monthly*, the *Edinburgh Review* and *Scribner's*. There were also, however, many novels by such authors as Charles Dickens, J. Fenimore Cooper, Jules Verne, and Horatio Alger, as well as their lesser-known contemporaries.

In its first decades the prison offered no formal educational program. As compulsory free public education was not yet established in the United States, few of the prisoners were able to read or write well, so the chaplain provided basic instruction in the three Rs. With the appointment of a full-time teacher in 1854, elementary education and bookkeeping, Spanish, and German courses were available. The teacher also wrote letters for inmates who could not do so themselves, and individually tutored a large number of inmates once a week. In theory, instruction had to take place in the cells; it was not until all pretense at continuing the separate system at Cherry Hill was dropped in the twentieth century that designated classrooms were finally built.

Labor

In the early nineteenth century prison reformers could not agree whether inmates should be required or even allowed to work during their sentence. By the time Cherry Hill opened in 1829, the issue was resolved, and state law specified that confinement should be at hard labor. However, officials at Cherry Hill were convinced that unrelieved solitary confinement during the first several days of an inmate's sentence would intimidate the prisoner (an opinion still echoed today, when prison work is regarded as a privilege and confinement without a job as punitive). The policy they developed was described in the first annual report of the prison:

When a convict first arrives, he is placed in a cell and left alone, without work and without any book. His mind can only operate on itself; generally, but few hours elapse before he petitions for something to do, and for a bible. No instance has occurred, in which such a petition has been delayed beyond a day or two. If the prisoner have a trade that can be pursued in his cell, he is put to work as a favour; as a reward for good behaviour, and as a favour, a bible is allowed him. If he have no trade, or one that cannot be pursued in his cell, he is allowed to choose one that can, and he is instructed by one of the overseers, all of whom are master workmen in the trades they respectively superintend and teach. Thus work, and moral and religious books, are regarded and received as favours, and are withheld as a punishment.[15]

Reviewing the policy's progress, the annual report also mentioned that the first prisoner at the penitentiary was instructed for four days in making shoes, which were sold to an outside agent.[16] Although there was opposition from labor unions to the sale of prison-made products, such goods were distributed in the community at prices comparable to those of goods outside.

Shoemaking and textile processes were typical activities in the early decades of the prison. Convicts were engaged in weaving, sewing, bleaching, and dyeing in their cells, which were sometimes double-sized to accommodate large equipment. Some exercise yards were covered to provide additional space for inmates to carry on their trades. Unlike other prisons, where outside firms used inmate labor and provided raw materials or marketing services, at Cherry Hill the officials had to purchase the raw materials, provide trade instruction, and then arrange for the sale and distribution of the manufactured goods. These activities were scaled back as organized labor began to lobby for laws limiting the sale of prison-made products.

Another occupation common in prisons in both Britain and the United States was picking oakum, or pounded hemp. This process involved separating single strands of hemp from used rope; when tarred, the product was used as caulking in wooden ships. In 1839 there were 159 prisoners engaged in weaving, 156 in shoemaking, 33 in picking oakum, and the rest either idle or engaged in maintenance or housekeeping tasks. As early as 1833, an official British observer noted prisoners working as carpenters, blacksmiths, stonecutters, and cooks.[17]

The general market for the prisoners' output of handmade shoes and woven products declined in the 1870s and 1880s as machine-made goods were manufactured more cheaply outside. Prisoners at the time were prohibited from using power machinery, leaving them at a competitive disadvantage. Woodworking and chairmaking, mainstays of production at mid-century, had all but died out by the time of the Civil War. In the 1880s prisoners were employed in chair caning, cigar making, printing colored labels for cigar-box lids, and manufacturing hosiery. Female prisoners were generally occupied in sewing, mending and making clothes, or caning chairs, usually working in pairs. Nonetheless, by the end of the century inmates at Cherry Hill were mostly idle, engaging only in repair work and the manufacture of clothing, shoes, blankets, or products used within the prison itself.

Authorities of the Auburn-system prisons claimed that inmates laboring in

Rotunda interior at Eastern State Penitentiary, 1890s. From Cassidy, 1897.

Cellblock seven corridor at Eastern State Penitentiary, 1890s, showing the ornate balustrade. From Cassidy, 1897.

IV Crucible of Good Intentions

workshops returned a profit that fully covered the costs of their incarceration. Annual reports of the Philadelphia prison periodically announced similar results. However, production at Cherry Hill was limited to prisoners working only in their cells and seldom met these goals. More often, annual reports tended to suggest that the reform of the inmates was more important than the mere pursuit of profits. One might reasonably surmise that this claim, which makes a virtue of necessity, was put forth when prison-made products were not finding a ready market.

Visitors to the Penitentiary

Prisoners' contacts with the outside world were severely restricted at Cherry Hill. Annual reports of the late nineteenth century indicate that one of the warden's duties was to talk with every prisoner at least twice a month. Each inmate was also visited by a clergyman of his denomination, a rabbi, or the official moral instructor. Representatives from the Pennsylvania Prison Society regularly visited all of the local prisons, including Cherry Hill, with each delegate assigned to a specific cellblock. Prison Society members were expected to visit individual inmates every two weeks. They observed prison conditions, such as lack of heat or prisoners out of their cells, and also heard grievances, but the minutes of the visiting committees of the Prison Society do not suggest that prisoners felt free to reveal abuses to them. Some members were more conscientious than others who visited infrequently, if ever, and rarely recorded unpleasant conditions or events. Michael Cassidy, who began working at the prison in 1861 and served as warden from 1881 to 1900, wrote that committee members came to Cherry Hill "every once in a while" to see the prisoners.[18]

At first prisoners were allowed no visits from family members or friends, but later, under special circumstances and with written permission from the Board of Inspectors, rare visits were granted. By the 1880s family visits to inmates were allowed once every three months. Likewise, letters, which were initially prohibited, later could be written if "supervised," that is, censored by the librarian, who also read the prisoners' incoming mail.

Inmates making hosiery in a cell at Eastern State Penitentiary, late nineteenth century. From Cassidy, 1897.

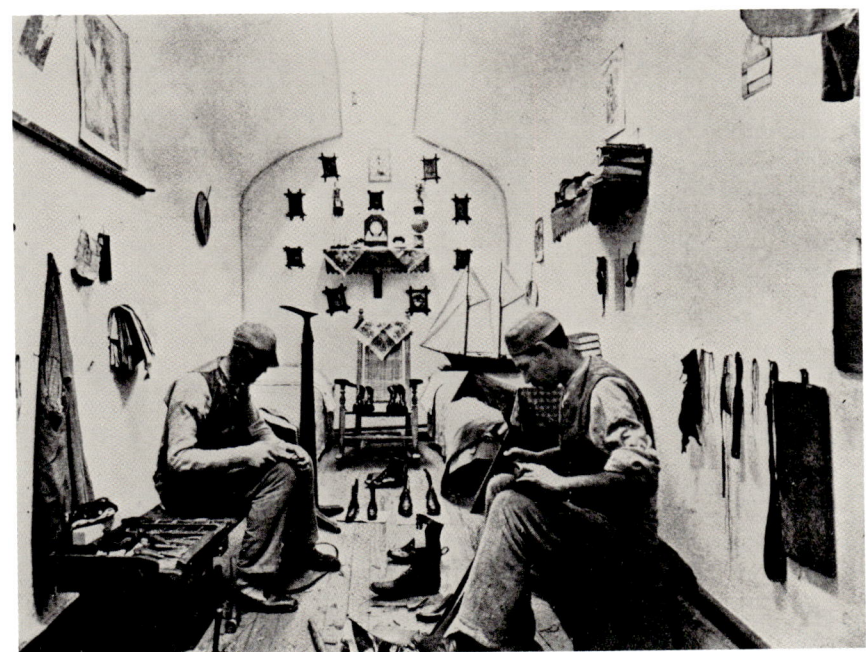

Inmates making shoes in a cell at Eastern State Penitentiary, late nineteenth century. From Cassidy, 1897.

The worldwide renown of the prison increased after a series of visits by prominent authors and government officials from abroad as well as from other states. Many European governments sent their representatives, sometimes even before the prison was completed, and Latin American countries and colonies such as Antigua, Jamaica, and Puerto Rico dispatched delegations in the mid-nineteenth century. Andrew Jackson, John Quincy Adams, the emperor of Brazil, several British Members of Parliament, and a number of state governors all signed the visitors' book.[19] The Marquis de Lafayette had visited the prison when it was still under construction. His response to seeing the massive front wall and towers and hearing of the system of solitary isolation was negative; he had been a prisoner of war in Austrian prisons for five years, three of them in solitary confinement. He was reported to have told a friend in Paris:

Of all the sufferings of my life, none have exceeded—none have equalled, that single oppression of being, for three whole years, asleep and awake, sitting or standing, exposed to the view of two eyes, watching my every motion, taking from my very thoughts every idea of privacy.[20]

The bulk of visitors, however, were ordinary people—local residents and schoolchildren, and tourists from all over the country, including Ottawas from Michigan and Menominees from Wisconsin.[21] As an attraction for travelers, Cherry Hill was said to rank with Niagara Falls and the national Capitol. In the early years the number of visitors was modest: in 1835 only about 1,100 entered; by 1839 there were 4,000 visitors. In 1859 Warden John Halloway reported that in the preceding five-year period over 40,000 people came. And in the decade from 1862 to 1872, Cherry Hill was visited by 114,440 sightseers.[22] Admission tickets were sold and regular hours for touring the penitentiary were posted. One may speculate that prison officials concluded that the deterrent effect on the public from viewing the prison justified what must have been considerable inconvenience involved in conducting the tours.

"A most dreadful, fearful place"

On March 8, 1842, Eastern State Penitentiary received its most well known but most unsettling visitor—the enormously popular young writer Charles Dickens.[23] Dickens was royally received wherever he went in the United States on his tour. Enthusiastic crowds pressed on him at every public appearance. Following the War of 1812 many Englishmen had traveled to the United States and written of their journeys. Often their books painted a negative picture of the new republic, much to the delight of conservatives at home. Dickens's original intention seems to have been to enlighten some of those views, but it cannot be said that he approached Eastern State Penitentiary with a completely open mind about solitary confinement.[24] It was to be a visit neither the author nor Philadelphians would soon forget.

Dickens was warmly welcomed at Cherry Hill. He had lunch with the inspectors and was quoted as saying that "the Falls of Niagara and your Penitentiary are two objects I might almost say I most wish to see."[25] He wrote to his

IV Crucible of Good Intentions

Admission ticket for Eastern State Penitentiary, c. 1835. The Library Company of Philadelphia.

friend and later biographer, John Forster: "Accordingly I passed the whole day in going from cell to cell, and conversing with the prisoners. Every facility was given me, and no constraint whatever imposed upon any man's free speech." He suggested that he told the officials of his reservations about their system and said: "All this, they took like men who were really anxious to have one's free opinion, and to do right. And we were very much pleased with each other, and parted in the friendliest way."[26]

In *American Notes for General Circulation*, published later that year, Dickens's tone is decidedly anti-American. Regarding prisons, Dickens wrote a scathing description of the Tombs in Manhattan, which also had been designed by Haviland. He mentioned Auburn and Sing Sing prisons in two sentences complimentary to the silent system, but he devoted nearly his entire chapter on Philadelphia—thirty pages in the early editions of the book—to his visit to Cherry Hill. His first characterization of the officials of the prison and himself as "pleased with each other" was certainly not evident in his published account:

In the outskirts, stands a great prison, called the Eastern Penitentiary: conducted on a plan peculiar to the state of Pennsylvania. The system here, is rigid, strict, and hopeless solitary confinement. I believe it, in its effects, to be cruel and wrong. . . . I am persuaded that those who devised this system of Prison Discipline, and those benevolent gentlemen who carry it into execution, do not know what it is that they are doing. . . . I hold this slow and daily tampering with the mysteries of the brain, to be immeasurably worse than any torture of the body: and because its ghastly signs and tokens are not so palpable to the eye and sense of touch as scars upon the flesh; because its wounds are not upon the surface, and it extorts few cries that human ears can hear; therefore I the more denounce it, as a secret punishment which slumbering humanity is not roused up to stay.[27]

Response to *American Notes* on both sides of the Atlantic was generally unfavorable. It struck some as "shallow, slipshod, and spiteful."[28] Reaction in the United States was particularly strong. Dickens seemed to have repaid American hospitality with a petty, critical book about the country and later a novel, *The Life and Adventures of Martin Chuzzlewit*, portraying the United States in highly unflattering terms.

The reaction to Dickens's book by the partisans of the Pennsylvania system was predictably indignant and did not abate for the rest of the nineteenth century. Controversy centered particularly on the cases of specific prisoners Dickens described so movingly in *American Notes*. One British author devoted an entire chapter in his book on prisons to "The Fictions of Dickens upon Solitary Confinement," taking the novelist's account case by case. He concluded that Dickens had apparently embellished his descriptions and made up one character.[29] In response to Dickens's account of his interviews with inmates, the Pennsylvania Prison Society asked the British consul-general for the State of Pennsylvania to interview the same convicts again.

Perhaps the most moving case raised by Dickens was that of "a German, . . . a more dejected, heart-broken, wretched creature, it would be difficult to imagine. I never saw such a picture of forlorn affliction and distress of mind. My heart bled for him."[30] He described the prisoner's tears and trembling hands. When the British consul later talked to the same man, he found him cheerful and in good health. "He is an ingenious and clever fellow but a great hypocrite, and evidently saw Mr. D's weak side."[31] This inmate was considered to be a troublemaker and eventually served nine sentences at Cherry Hill and five at other prisons. When he was eighty years old and living on the street, he returned to the prison and begged to be taken in. He died soon after in the penitentiary.[32]

The apparently willful inaccuracy of Dickens's account continued to provoke a heated response nearly fifty years later, when an article, "Charles Dickens' Prison Fictions," written by William Tallack of the Howard Association—a London prisoners' welfare organization—was published in the Pennsylvania Prison

Marcus Stone (1840–1921), *The Solitary Prisoner*, 1870s. Engraving. From Charles Dickens, *Pictures from Italy and American Notes for General Circulation* (Boston: James Osgood and Co., 1875).

Society *Journal of Prison Discipline* in 1894. Tallack's article was reissued in pamphlet form in Britain by the association.[33] From the vantage point of the present, it is clear that Dickens did recognize the inherent cruelty of the separate system, even from his brief visit to Cherry Hill. But, as an observer he was far from objective and failed to note the different cruelties in other prisons. Dickens also criticized Pentonville, the prototype London prison modeled after Cherry Hill, without ever having stepped inside its gates.[34]

Health of the Prisoners

Prisons have never been healthy places, but when Cherry Hill was built its system of confinement in cells posed new problems for the maintenance of the prisoners' physical and mental health. Medical care in the penitentiary at first was provided by a physician and one or more male nurses. One of the prisoners, a former physician, was even put to work as a nurse in such a way that other inmates should not learn his true status. A common infirmary and an apothecary's shop were situated on the second floor of the front building when the prison opened. Shortly afterward prisoners were treated in special hospital cells in cellblock two and later in cellblock three, where the hospital remained for the rest of the century.

The value of personal hygiene was not lost on Cherry Hill's administrators; although the early arrangements for bathing were makeshift, by 1845 several cells had been converted to provide hot baths. Inmates wearing hoods would be brought to bathe individually every two or three weeks. (This was not regarded as infrequent; a young man wrote to a newspaper in 1835: "I have been in the habit during the past winter of taking a warm bath every three weeks. Is this too often to follow the year round?"[35]) In the summer, bathing took place outside, presumably with unheated water. By the end of the century inmates had baths weekly, and personal hygiene was probably better than in the homes of most of the city's poor, who lacked bathroom tubs and running hot water.

Personal cleanliness was only one concern of prison administrators. Even with Haviland's innovations in central heating, ventilation, and plumbing, the prison was cold, damp, and foul. In 1849 Prison Society visitors reported that prisoners had to wrap themselves in their blankets and pace up and down their cells to keep warm. Toilets were supposed to be flushed once a day (a practice still in effect at the turn of the century), but scarcity of water sometimes made even that impossible; in 1852 the pipes were flushed only two or three times a week.

Although inmates were supposed to be allowed to use their exercise yards for an hour a day, in practice this time was often not allotted. In the 1840s a Prison Society official noted that in some cellblocks, the time in the yard was only thirty minutes a day, and when the weather was poor even this was not possible.[36] In 1887 a gymnasium was built, in an effort to combat tuberculosis through exercise. Prisoners were brought in six at a time, wearing face masks.

The medical records and annual reports from Cherry Hill also reveal the Victorian-era preoccupation of the administrators with the "solitary vice." Most, but not all, doctors of the period regarded masturbation as leading inevitably to serious medical or mental consequences. Annual reports of the prison physician frequently refer to masturbation: "[Number] 6694, white male, aged 25, is recorded as having died of *asthma*, produced by masturbation," "7032, white male, aged 17, died of *debility*.... Persistent masturbation was the sole cause of his death."[37] The annual report of 1838 noted eighteen cases of "insanity," twelve of which were confidently ascribed to the practice. In 1889 Warden Cassidy described a prisoner who committed suicide by setting fire to his cell and inhaling the smoke. His demise was said to have been caused by "excessive masturbation."[38]

William White, the prison physician in 1875, took a more moderate view of the issue. He surmised that many of the prison's inmates identified as "confirmed onanists" had a predisposition due to prior illness or heredity and suggested that there were others "who are known to indulge in this habit more or less frequently . . . who have never evinced any decided unsoundness whatever."[39] In the 1876 annual report Dr. White presented three pages of tables outlining data on the family backgrounds of known masturbators. While the doctor's efforts may have been enlightened, it is also more than likely that officials at Cherry Hill were eager to cite any mitigating factors in their larger attempt to disclaim responsibility for nearly all the ills developed by inmates incarcerated at the prison.

Detractors of the Pennsylvania system claimed that physical and mental deterioration was the inevitable consequence of separate confinement. *The Times* (London), which had taken an editorial position opposing the Pennsylvania system in the 1840s, was not the first to characterize the Cherry Hill regimen as "*maniac-making.*"[40] Counterclaims charged that the conditions noted in many prisoners were preexisting. As early as 1832 the prison physician, Dr. Bache, wrote:

Prisoner No. 112 was received on the 16th of February 1832, apparently well. But the appearance of good health proved fallacious; for after the lapse of a month, he began to show symptoms of aberration of mind, and on the 28th of March, less than six weeks after his reception, he was in a state of such violent mental excitement, as to require to be placed in a dark cell. His insanity continued, with but an unimportant abatement in April, until the 26th of May, when he died. These facts prove conclusively, that this prisoner, though apparently well on admission, was strongly predisposed to mania, and on the verge of an attack of that disease.[41]

Although there seems to have been a high proportion of mentally ill prisoners in the penitentiary, it is important to note that diagnosis was not well developed and criminal insanity and mental deficiency not clearly identified in the nineteenth century. Prisons were the dumping ground for a significant number of mentally ill men and women, undoubtedly due to the dearth of public facilities to care for the criminally insane. Many of them came through the courts into prisons in all parts of the country in the middle of the last century.[42] In the following decades, as public mental institutions and hospitals for the criminally insane were opened, fewer disturbed individuals were sent to Cherry Hill, and the charges that the separate system itself caused mental derangement in prisoners seem to have dwindled in public discourse about the regimen. And long before American clinicians became interested in the link between solitary confinement and mental illness, its use in Eastern State Penitentiary had been discontinued except as punishment for rule infractions.[43]

In response to concerns about the effect of separate confinement on inmates' health, careful records were kept at Cherry Hill, categorizing the condition of prisoners at admission and again at discharge. The 1832 annual report reveals the subjective and vague classificatory terms used, ranging from "not robust" and "imperfect" to "insane." One prisoner who was "not good" when received was "improved" when discharged; one who was "robust" on entering was in an "excellent" state of health when he left. Official judgments of the physical and mental health of those admitted to the prison seem to have been unduly pessimistic to shield the institution from later accusations of having caused illnesses during incarceration. For example, in 1875 the prison physician stated that of the 801 convicts who had been received during that year, 59 percent had arrived in impaired mental and physical health or were prone to develop diseases from inherited defects.[44] From 1891 to 1895, there were 337 convicts declared insane or in impaired mental health admitted to Cherry Hill and 241 discharged.

The accusations of the unhealthy consequences of separate confinement led officials repeatedly to make public statements of reassurance that the system had no deleterious effects on those confined. Mortality rates at Cherry Hill and at what officials regarded as the best of the rival congregate prisons were compared, and the claim was made that the rates were equal. Figures were also gathered to support the hypothesis that inmates incarcerated for long periods at Cherry Hill had no higher mortality rates than did those serving shorter sentences.

During an outbreak of typhoid fever in 1870, which resulted in several deaths at the prison, the city water supply, taken directly from the polluted Schuylkill River, was held to be contaminated, and the prison provided distilled water for drinking until the situation was corrected. Officials often denied that disciplinary confinement in "dark cells" contributed to tuberculosis and blamed a predisposition, as they had for mental illness. In short, infirmities of all kinds among prisoners were ascribed to their having entered the prison in poor health or bearing inherited tendencies toward specific diseases. Particularly in the nineteenth century, the men and women who were sentenced to the penitentiary had been rarely treated by physicians on the outside, and they may well have suffered from dietary deficiencies and other undiagnosed medical problems.

Maintaining Discipline

A prison routine in which most inmates were confined to their cells twenty-four hours a day provided few opportunities to violate rules, but inevitably there were infractions. They varied from the trivial to the very serious: a failure to clean eating utensils or cells was a minor violation; making noise in the cell and trying to communicate with fellow prisoners were more significant. From there, misdeeds went up the scale from refusing to work, destroying cell equipment, assaulting an overseer or the warden, or attempting to escape, to injuring or killing a fellow prisoner or a guard.

Most observers agreed that physical punishments at Cherry Hill were mild in comparison to other prison systems of the time. Corporal punishment was still very much a part of mid-nineteenth-century life in the United States; in schools, orphanages, asylums, and on navy and merchant ships, flogging was a common practice. In their survey of American prisons in 1831, Tocqueville and Beaumont claimed that of all state penitentiaries only Philadelphia's did not use the lash; nevertheless, although it was alleged that there was no corporal punishment, investigations ordered by the state legislature in 1834–35 and 1897 showed otherwise.

The mildest punishment in the early decades was probably confinement to one's cell without work, or denial of time in the exercise yard. There might also be a modest reduction in diet for one or more weeks, or no meat for three days. More serious punishment consisted of time in the "dungeon," one of the dark cells with blocked skylights and none of the normal furnishings, not even a bed. Here the inmate might be placed in irons and restricted to half a pound of bread and water for up to seven days, a punishment only the warden could order. Inmates were provided with a single blanket in these punishment cells, even in the coldest weather, and sometimes this was taken away. In some cases the bread and water regimen was cruelly extended. The 1834–35 investigation described a sixteen-year-old prisoner confined in the dark cell for forty-two days, supposedly with no food. Checking him, the keeper saw that the inmate was delirious and, violating the rules, gave him some bread. The next day the keeper reported the matter to the prison physician, who verified the condition of the prisoner, releasing him only after making a second report. The keeper involved in this incident testified before the Board of Inspectors and was fired by the warden.[45]

There were other severe punishments at Cherry Hill in the early years. One was the "shower bath," not uncommon in prisons at the time. The 1834–35 investigative report cited the case of a young horse-thief named Seneca Plimly, who in frigid weather was stripped to the waist and tied by the wrists to the wall of his exercise yard, then doused with buckets of water while ice formed on his hair and body.[46]

Another punishment uncovered in the 1834–35 investigation was the "Mad Chair" or "Tranquilizing Chair," a device used to calm mental patients and reputedly invented by Benjamin Rush. The prisoner was held in the chair by chains, leather straps, and locks so that he was immobilized. Prisoners were sometimes beaten while in the chair, and when restrained for long periods, their legs would become severely swollen. One inmate was put in the chair for making threats against the doctor.[47]

The iron gag was a five-inch-long device that fitted over the prisoner's tongue. One's hands were put in leather gloves and crossed behind the back; chains on the gloves were linked to the gag. By all accounts this punishment was extremely painful and caused injury and bleeding. One prisoner, Matthias Maccumsey, died while subjected to the gag. The cause of his death was listed as "apoplexy," and although the case was known to the public, there was no investigation.[48]

Straitjackets were also used for punishment. When one was restrictively laced in this canvas device, originally used in mental hospitals, the neck and face could become black and the hands numb.

After the 1834–35 investigation, most of these severe punishments were abandoned; although there were still dark cells in the 1870s, their use supposedly was

IV Crucible of Good Intentions

Iron gag, one of the punishments used at Eastern State Penitentiary, 1830s. Wood engraving. From Thomas B. McElwee, *A Concise History of the Eastern Penitentiary of Pennsylvania* (Philadelphia: Neall and Massey, 1835).

Tranquilizing chair, 1830s. Wood engraving.

Straitjacket, 1830s. Wood engraving.

discontinued. A policeman's baton, or billy club, was kept in each cellblock, but infrequently used. Lesser punishments, such as the denial of work, the revocation of exercise-yard privileges, and a reduced diet, persisted and, in fact, remained common in most prisons in the United States through the mid-twentieth century.[49]

Escapes

Haviland designed a prison he thought would be secure from escapes, particularly since inmates were to be continually confined to their cells. The surrounding wall, thirty feet high, was topped with an inclined coping that projected two feet from the inner surface to hinder attempts to climb over it. The radial plan also afforded excellent surveillance of the prison. All inmates and guards walking through the prison corridors could be observed by officers stationed in the central rotunda. From the exterior balcony on the second level of the center building some of the yards and open spaces of the prison enclosure could be seen, and from a small balcony surrounding the lantern, or topmost part of the center tower, officers could survey the yards and roofs of the entire prison. So that nothing would obscure the view of the prison from the center, Haviland avoided filling the space between the cellblocks with buildings; over time, however, the prison grounds inevitably became cluttered with structures as the increasing number of prisoners required additional accommodations and changing routines called for new facilities.

To make it easier for guards to see on their patrols the building was well lighted. The cells and the corridors were originally lit with candles or lamps using fish or whale oil. It is not known if there was any exterior lighting in the early days, but by 1856 gas lines had been installed, and in addition to jets in each cell and in the corridors, there were eight exterior gas lights with large reflectors. Electricity came to the prison in 1889.

The prison that appeared to be a fortress was breached within three years of its opening. The first escape was by the prison baker, who served as a waiter in the warden's residence. He entered the warden's quarters on a Sunday, climbed to the roof, tied a bedcord to a stick he placed in the facade crenelations, and lowered himself to the ground, taking with him a razor, some clothing, and silverware belonging to the warden. He was captured and returned to the prison, but several years later escaped again in a similar fashion. Other prisoners went out over the wall with the aid of handmade ladders and ropes. One prisoner wove a rope out of stocking yarn and thread used for making shoes and fastened it to the top of the wall with a hook.

Some inmates chose less arduous ways of leaving. One, who had been working as a stonecutter, donned a workman's hat and sauntered out the front gate with the free laborers on their way to breakfast. Through the years a number of prisoners walked out the front door disguised as civilians, having made their own overcoats or suits. One inmate found his corridor door and the front gate unlocked and simply walked out. In 1877 a prisoner hid himself in an empty molasses barrel and was carted away. Some escape attempts were made by digging under the cell floors, and small groups of prisoners went out through the sewer in 1871 and 1877. These early escapes were rarely noted in the prison's official annual reports, but were reported in local newspapers.

Scandals

Public institutions rarely avoid accusations of scandalous conduct. At Eastern State Penitentiary such charges were not long in coming. Four years after the prison was opened several employees went to the president of the Board of Inspectors, Judge Charles Coxe, with accounts of improprieties. Although testimony was taken, apparently no action followed. Subsequently, the attorney general of Pennsylvania reviewed the testimony and recommended that an investigation of the prison be carried out. Hearings in front of a joint legislative committee were begun in Philadelphia in December 1834. The first charge involved:

Practices and manners among the officers, agents and females, licentious and immoral; attested by indecent conversations, gross personal familiarities, sexual intercourse, and the existence of a filthy [venereal] disease; generally known to and participated in by the Warden, one John Halloway [the prison clerk], one Richard Blundin [an overseer] and his wife, and others unknown.[50]

There were accusations of wild parties and drinking late at night in the front building. Most of the trouble seemed to center on Mrs. Blundin. She was reported to be vulgar and unrestrained, and reputedly had sexual relations with the warden, several inmates, and others.[51] Testimony was given about her carrying eggs, roast beef, ham, apple butter, and preserves to an inmate's cell. Her evening entertainments, billed as "quilting parties," went on until late at night and involved excessive drinking. The male and female prisoners who assisted at her parties or the warden's did not wear masks.

The second charge involved embezzlement and misuse of public property to the personal advantage of various people connected with the prison, particularly members of the Board of Inspectors and the warden. The ubiquitous Mrs. Blundin had been seen carrying food and other provisions out the front gate. She also boarded some prison staff and construction workers in her quarters, presumably using state provisions.

The third charge involved the infliction of cruel and unusual punishment on the prisoners. The cases of Seneca Plimly and Matthias Maccumsey were presented in detail, but the committee members were not greatly disturbed by them, noting that the iron gag had been used at the Walnut Street Jail and was still used in the United States Navy, and that subjecting people to straitjackets and cold-water showers was common in other prisons and mental asylums in the state.

The last charge involved the use of prisoners for various maintenance and housekeeping duties outside their cells. The committee was presented with testimony that some male and female prisoners did indeed have freedom to walk about the prison or to converse with other prisoners and free workmen. Testimony revealed that inmates sometimes made candy with the overseers, one took care of a horse and a cow on the premises, others carried mortar and stone for the construction workers, and some did Mrs. Blundin's washing. One prisoner, nicknamed "The General," would go, unaccompanied by an overseer, from one end of the cellblock to the other, attending to the furnaces in the tunnels. Warden Wood admitted that most of these lapses in policy had indeed taken place out of expediency, and the members of the committee requested that such practices stop once construction on the cellblocks was completed.

The legislative committee, with one exception, generally reaffirmed their confidence in the Board of Inspectors and in Warden Wood, making a few modest suggestions and mild reprimands. By this time Mrs. Blundin was already gone, so no action could be taken in respect to her behavior. Afterward, the warden fired several of the prison staff who had testified. Judge Coxe resigned his post as president of the board in frustration over the imperfections of the system. His letter of resignation, written before the investigation had been carried out, stated in part: "Satisfied that abuses exist . . . to an alarming extent, and that all efforts on my part . . . to remove them have been fruitless I can no longer allow my name to be used to authenticate acts of the Board."[52]

In 1897 another investigation of the penitentiary was initiated after Philadelphia Judge James Gordon heard details of a grand jury report concerning filthy conditions in the cells, callous treatment of the mentally ill, and brutality and neglect. One inmate was said to have been tied to steam pipes in his cell and was burned, another to have died as the result of a beating. The Board of Inspectors denied these accusations and asked for a legislative investigation to clear the

View of the original seven wings and rotunda from the front tower at Eastern State Penitentiary, c. 1870. From Vaux, 1872.

South Hall of State Prison, Auburn, New York, the original prison of the rival Auburn system, as it appeared in the 1940s.

names of the prison officials. Warden Cassidy defended his administration, and the investigation absolved the prison staff of any wrongdoing.[53]

Other Prisons

Conditions at Eastern State Penitentiary in the nineteenth century must be judged against those in other prisons in the United States at the time. Most prisons modeled their facilities and regimens after the Auburn and Sing Sing prisons in New York State. Cells in these prisons invariably were small: the cells at Sing Sing were three feet three inches wide and seven feet long, and those at Kingston Penitentiary in Ontario were two feet six inches by six feet six inches. The bed filled the entire cell and was stored swung up against the wall.

Cells everywhere were poorly ventilated and cold, with damp walls or floors. At Auburn and Sing Sing prisons the only sources of heat were a few stoves located at the ends of the cellblocks. Plumbing in the cells, whether a water tap or a toilet, was rare; inmates usually had a bucket for a sink and another for a toilet. At Auburn the only natural light in a cell was that penetrating a heavy iron latticework door set in a deeply recessed doorway.

The Virginia Penitentiary in Richmond, designed by the architect of the Capitol, Benjamin Henry Latrobe, had windowless oak doors to the cells. These cells had no heating or plumbing. In the Maine State Prison at Thomaston, opened in the 1820s, the cells were below ground and inmates entered by a ladder through a two-foot-square opening; the hatch was locked after the ladder was pulled up.

The so-called silent or Auburn system could scarcely be described as more humane than the separate system developed at Eastern State Penitentiary. From the time a prisoner entered a facility such as Sing Sing, a concerted effort was made to subdue his will. There, as nearly everywhere, prisoners were dressed in black-and-white-striped uniforms, and they were subjected to a routine calculated to control them at all times. At Auburn the morning bell rang once at 6 a.m. The inmates got up and the guards shouted, "Tubs, cans, and kids." "Tubs" were used instead of the cell toilets found at Cherry Hill; "cans" contained the inmates' water supply; "kids" were the wooden bowls that had been used for the previous evening's meal. Another bell rang and the inmates stepped in unison from their cells to the balconies on each of the five levels of cells. On a further order, the inmates marched. Breakfast was at 7 a.m. The inmates would file into the dining room and sit down to eat at the sound of a bell; after twenty to thirty minutes another bell would sound and they would file out. The routine was repeated at noon. The workday ended at 4:30 p.m. Inmates were then marched to the courtyard, where they were issued their "tubs, cans, and kids," and to the mess hall, where they received their evening meal to carry back to their cells. At 5:30 p.m., after the chaplain had conducted a service, they were allowed to eat their food, now cold. Inmates were moved, as at other Auburn-type prisons, in a lockstep formation: usually in single file, with the right hand on the shoulder of the person ahead of them. Their heads were to remain fixed in the direction of the officer. Absolute silence was required unless addressing a staff member. The

IV CRUCIBLE OF GOOD INTENTIONS

Inmates from Sing Sing prison, Ossining, New York, nineteenth century.

workshops, which could also be observed through peepholes, were arranged so that inmates did not face each other. They were not allowed to speak.⁵⁴

Such a system, with inmates out of their cells during the daytime, offered more opportunities to violate rules. Punishment was swift and severe. At Auburn, as at most prisons except Cherry Hill, the usual form of punishment was flogging as a matter of open, official policy, carried out on the spot if the guard saw fit. Warden Elam Lynds of Auburn, one of the initiators of the congregate system, used a rawhide whip with six separate strands. Five hundred blows were sometimes administered to the bare backs of offenders. Inmates considered insane were not exempted. Warden Lynds told Tocqueville and Beaumont during their mission to observe American prisons: "I consider it impossible to govern a large prison without a whip."⁵⁵ In one case of brutal whipping that came before a local New York court, the judge was moved to state:

*That the welfare of society, as well as the reformation of the convicts, required that they should feel that they were in reality, the slaves of the state. . . . That they should most deeply feel the awful degradation and misery, to which their vicious courses had reduced them.*⁵⁶

Other punishments, such as those described as occasionally taking place at Cherry Hill, were routine in prisons in the United States. In Virginia and elsewhere male or female prisoners might be fitted with a steel headpiece that forced a metal strip or gag in their mouths. In 1877 an investigation of practices in a juvenile reform school in Massachusetts found that the gag was still in use. Straitjackets were employed there, as at Auburn, and boys were confined in a sweatbox with dimensions that did not allow them to move, so that after several hours their limbs began to swell. The boys were also subjected to solitary confinement in dark cells where they were manacled to the floor and given only bread and water for as long as a month.⁵⁷

The idealism held to by the Philadelphia reformers, even for the day-to-day running of Cherry Hill, was decidedly lacking in many American penal establishments, especially at Auburn and Sing Sing. When Warden Lynds was asked by Tocqueville and Beaumont if he believed in the reform of a great number of his prisoners, he replied: "We must understand each other; I do not believe in a *complete* reform, except with young delinquents. Nothing, in my opinion, is rarer than to see a convict of mature age become a religious and virtuous man." When asked by what criterion he judged a prisoner to have reformed, he responded: "Nothing. If it were necessary to

Noble Ideas Collide with Reality

David Johnston Kennedy (1816/17–1898), *Black Maria, Prison Van*, 1837. Watercolor, 6 x 5". Historical Society of Pennsylvania.

mention a prognostic, I would even say that the prisoner who conducts himself well, will probably return to his former habits, when set free."[58] Lynds's disdain for idealistic goals of reform achieved during imprisonment was a far cry from the exalted hopes and the philosophy of treatment associated with the creators of Cherry Hill.

Two Systems

All through the century proponents of the two competing systems fiercely defended their views on imprisonment. Neither side ever admitted publicly that they may not have been on the right track, neither acknowledged the considerable flaws in the everyday working of their respective prisons. At Cherry Hill there were almost never enough cells or enough money to hire the workers needed to allow the system to operate in its pure form. When the ambiguous new term "individual treatment" first appeared in public policy statements by officials of Eastern State Penitentiary in 1872, what it implied (although this was never stated) was that the separation of prisoners from one another could no longer be maintained, even in its imperfect form. Yet, in the 1896 annual report of the prison, noting that European countries were building prisons for the separate system, the Prison Inspectors would still predict that "within a comparatively short period the congregate [Auburn] method will have been abandoned everywhere, except within those American states that still consider it advisable to convert their prisons into factories."[59]

The supporters of the Cherry Hill system nevertheless sounded increasingly anachronistic as penological trends in the United States soon passed both systems by. Cherry Hill, the sole exemplar of the system of separation in the United States, was soon to capitulate. Within a few years the only vestige of its original idealistic purpose was its architecture.

Did Eastern State Penitentiary work better than prisons patterned after Auburn and Sing Sing? Recidivism would be a revealing index of successful reform, but determining the rate of recidivism of released prisoners in the nineteenth century, before the advent of fingerprinting and centralized criminal recordkeeping, is difficult. In financial terms, neither system fulfilled the dream of its founders to reduce the taxpayers' burden, although Cherry Hill was always more expensive to run.

It was certainly the case that many prisoners, especially those vulnerable in body or mind, were harmed mentally or physically by their solitary existence in the Philadelphia prison. Other sorts of harm occurred in the congregate prisons elsewhere. Indeed, a choice between the corrosiveness of enforced isolation and the physical violence and calculated tyranny of routines in other prisons would have been a difficult one, had inmates been given the opportunity to make it.

Strangeways Prison, Manchester, England, 1865–68.

Cherry Hill: Model for the World

NORMAN JOHNSTON

Plate showing Eastern State Penitentiary, from a dessert service, c.1838–42, with views of Philadelphia. Made at the Rihouet factory, Paris (1818–89). Hard-paste porcelain, diameter 8⅜". Philadelphia Museum of Art. Gift of Mrs. John Penn Brock.

If the experiment with the Pennsylvania system at Eastern State Penitentiary was a failure—and it was ultimately regarded as such in the United States—the theory continued to have an enormous appeal to many prison reformers. In the early days, before the theory's promise had been seriously eroded by contact with reality, penologists around the world regarded Eastern State Penitentiary—known by many as Cherry Hill—as the perfect prison. Its construction caused a sensation. Soon after the first three cellblocks were finished, the governments of Great Britain, France, Prussia, Russia, Belgium, Spain, Brazil, Chile, China, and other nations began sending representatives to evaluate the rival prison regimens in New York and Pennsylvania. Almost without exception, international reports favored the latter, and it is probable that the high quality of Haviland's architecture was an important factor in the widespread acceptance of the Pennsylvania system.

Although it was Eastern State Penitentiary that became the primary target in the controversy over the two systems, and the prison most often mentioned in penological writings, Haviland's New Jersey State Prison, erected in Trenton in the 1830s, was also to influence prison design worldwide. Constructed after Eastern State Penitentiary, the Trenton prison profited from the example of its Philadelphia counterpart. The New Jersey State Prison consisted of five wings radiating in a half-circle from an inspection room, an arrangement that centralized the administrative and service functions at the hub. There were no attached exercise yards at the Trenton prison.

Influence on Prisons in the United States

In the United States in the nineteenth century, with its chronic labor shortages, a prison built and operated at great cost that could not efficiently utilize or realize profits from the labor of its inmates was simply unacceptable. As a consequence the adoption of the Pennsylvania system by other states was limited, and for this

V Crucible of Good Intentions

plans in the United States rather than their own earlier buildings that provided the models for subsequent British prisons.

In the early 1830s the British government commissioned Sir William Crawford to investigate state prisons in the United States "with a view to ascertain the practicability and expediency of applying the respective systems on which they are governed, or any parts thereof, to the prisons of this country."[3] In 1834 the Home Office published his elaborate report, which included plans of the most important penitentiaries and an unequivocal recommendation that the system of separate confinement in force at Cherry Hill become official policy in Britain. A prototype prison was to be built in London, and Haviland submitted plans. The Model Prison, known as Pentonville, was nevertheless designed and built by Sir Charles Barry and an army engineer, Joshua Jebb, who later became Surveyor General of Prisons. Opened in 1842, the prison housed convicts in strict isolation before their transport to penal colonies in Australia or elsewhere. Beginning in 1848, reports of physical and mental health problems at Pentonville resulted in authorities' shortening the terms to be served in isolation to twelve months. Further dilution of the system occurred in subsequent years, although the use of isolation in cells continued into the 1940s.

Despite the controversies raging in England, as in the United States, over the efficacy of the separate system, British engineers and architects continued to accept Haviland's radial designs wholeheartedly, constructing prisons with two or more wings joined to a central rotunda. However, they criticized the lack of facilities for religious instruction and included in their prisons chapels with individual cubicles arranged so each inmate could see and hear the chaplain but remain isolated from his fellow prisoners. These stall chapels became an almost universal feature of European prisons in the nineteenth century. British and Continental architects also introduced circular structures with pie-wedge enclosures around a guard's central cubicle to separate inmates during exercise, rather than building individual exercise yards as at Cherry Hill. Later, circular exercise areas in an open yard were laid out, where inmates were marched while masked and chained together.

Following the construction of Pentonville in London, British prisons were built or rebuilt at a rapid rate.[4] At least thirty radial prisons were erected before the end of the nineteenth century. In effect, the multiwing design that evolved from Haviland's plans at Philadelphia and Trenton became the prototype for most British prisons up to the first decade of the twentieth century.

In the British colonies, radial prisons were erected in Canada, Australia, Malta, South Africa, Burma, New Zealand, and Hong Kong. In Canada, for example, the first of the reform prisons, built in the shape of a Greek cross with an enormous, domed central rotunda, was opened in Kingston, Ontario, in 1835. Most of the penitentiaries built in the nineteenth century in Canada were radial. Even in 1971 when Millhaven prison was opened as a maximum-security facility, its plan featured nine cell corridors radiating from four inspection hubs.

Bordeaux provincial jail, near Montreal, Canada, 1908–13.

Carabanchel prison, Madrid, opened in 1954.

The Continent Falls in Line

The countries of Continental Europe also experienced a surge in new prison construction. The Prussian government appointed a prominent expert on prison matters, Dr. Nicolaus Julius, to study American prisons in 1834. He returned from his visit to the United States a strong partisan of the Pennsylvania system and its architecture. In 1841 King Friedrich Wilhelm IV visited the yet-unfinished Pentonville in England. He not only admired the construction but was also convinced of the value of solitary confinement.[5] Subsequently, a new model prison designed by Karl Busse was begun in Berlin in 1844 on the Trenton or Pentonville pattern. Over forty radial prisons were eventually erected in the German states before 1910. While the architecture was consistent, the official policy on isolation in the nineteenth century was not: some prisons were run on the Pennsylvania system, some on the congregate system, and some made little effort to prevent prisoners from associating with one another. The Pennsylvania system, although further modified in the twentieth century by the establishment of a two-year limit for terms spent in isolation, remained in use in some German prisons until newer American penological practices were instituted during the Allied occupation after World War II.[6]

Belgium completely replaced its old prisons in the last half of the nineteenth century, largely through the untiring efforts of one man, Edouard Ducpétiaux. At the age of 26, he was named head of the prison system and long remained in that position, until his death in 1868. At first he espoused the Auburn system but, concluding that its results were unsatisfactory in Belgium, reversed

V

CRUCIBLE OF GOOD INTENTIONS

official policy in favor of the Pennsylvania system. During his administration, prisons were rebuilt with the requirement that all buildings for prisoners be in direct communication with a central observatory. Some, like those at Antwerp, Audenarde, and Charleroi, were V-shaped like Haviland's second Western Penitentiary at Pittsburgh; others, such as the large prison at Forest near Brussels, were in an X form. Still others, like Louvain and St. Giles, consisted of five or six wings radiating from a central rotunda. All but three of the more than twenty new Belgian prisons were radial. The Pennsylvania system retained its pristine severity in Belgium as long as in any other country. Some changes were enacted in the early years of the twentieth century and separate confinement was no longer regarded as the sole approach, but separate cubicles in the chapels, face masks, and individual exercise enclosures remained in use until after World War I.

Interest in prison reform came early to Spain, but, for financial reasons, new prisons began to be constructed later than in many other European countries. A Spanish translation of Duc F.-A.-F. de la Rochefoucauld-Liancourt's *Des Prisons de Philadelphie* became available in 1801, and the publications of John Howard and other prison reformers were routinely translated. In 1835 Ramón de la Sagra was commissioned to visit American and European prisons, and later he published an atlas of plans, many of them radial. It was not until 1859, however, that Spain's first radial prison with individual cells was built, in Vitoria, and in 1877 a model prison was begun in Madrid with plans by Tomás Aranguren. As in most later Spanish prisons, the radiating wings were tapered so that when cell doors were fastened slightly ajar inmates could observe mass conducted at an elevated altar in the central rotunda. Of the prisons, large and small, built in Spain, almost all—nearly forty—were on the radial plan. The largest prison built in the twentieth century is the Madrid provincial prison in Carabanchel, which opened in 1954, replacing the original model prison destroyed in the Spanish Civil War.

France, bedeviled by revolutions, disastrous wars, and political and economic instability from the late eighteenth century through most of the nineteenth century, showed the earliest interest in American prisons. The first foreign-language publication on Philadelphia's innovations in prison reform had been La Rochefoucauld-Liancourt's report of 1796. In the 1830s the French government sent two distinguished groups to America to report on prison reforms. The first group had been led by Gustave de Beaumont and Alexis de Tocqueville, writing their report in 1833.[7] A few years later Frédéric-Auguste Demetz, later to found the famous Mettray Colony for delinquent boys, and Guillaume-Abel Blouet, a government architect, also visited the United States. In 1837 their official report included a careful description of both the Auburn and the Pennsylvania systems as well as detailed plans of state prisons, particularly those of Pennsylvania, which the French government favored.[8]

The first large, cellular prison in France to be modeled after Cherry Hill was Mazas prison (1843–50) in Paris, a six-wing radial facility designed by Jean-François Lecointe and Emile Gilbert to hold convicts before the most serious offenders were assigned to penal colonies. Gilbert had worked under G.-A. Blouet, who admired Haviland's designs. Over

Individual exercise yards at Karlskrona prison, Sweden, 1851, used to isolate prisoners when exercising outside their cells.

Gothic-inspired gate of Kagoshima prison, Japan, 1908.

the next fifty years, a number of detention facilities were built on the radial plan.⁹ However, as France did not have a strong central government administering prisons, no consistent architectural policy prevailed in the nineteenth century. Although the twentieth century saw different kinds of prisons being constructed, in 1968 at Fleury Mérogis, near Paris, a prison for 2,900 inmates was opened with six three-wing radial groups of cellblocks.

In Italy reforms in the nineteenth century also developed slowly due to the lack of resources or a strong central government. Rather than building anew, Italian authorities frequently adapted existing fortresses or castles for prison use, as was occurring in France and eastern Europe. Before unification, the rulers of the individual states demonstrated little interest in prison reform. The Pennsylvania system was generally not as well received in Italy as it was in Switzerland and Germany.¹⁰ Although the first of the new prisons was established in Palermo (1834–40), it was the northern states that had the means and inclination to build. In Turin, Milan, and Rome, large-scale prisons based on the Cherry Hill plan were erected after 1840. In the twentieth century other configurations were more commonly used for prisons, particularly parallel cellblocks connected by a central corridor at right angles. However, in 1970 Rebibbia prison was built in Rome, consisting of three-wing radial clusters of cellblocks—one of the most recent examples of classic radial design.

Interest in prison reform began early in the nineteenth century in Russia. John Howard's works sold as many copies in St. Petersburg as in London.¹¹ A prison society was formed in Russia that researched ideas and model plans from western Europe and the United States. The Russian minister had visited John Haviland and was later furnished with a set of plans. In spite of these strong reform tendencies, only a handful of new structures were built in Russia until the late nineteenth century. The first cellular prison opened in St. Petersburg in 1880. Four years later in that city a new central facility, known as Kresty (cross) prison, was begun, consisting of two cruciform, five-story cellblocks. Although other prisons were built on a cross or V plan, Russia continued to reuse such structures as monasteries for incarceration well into the twentieth century.

The few large prisons that were built in other countries of western Europe were almost always patterned after Cherry Hill, Trenton, or Pentonville. Prison reform in Sweden, for example, began with the publication in 1840 of a treatise by Crown Prince Oskar, which was later translated into French, German, Norwegian, and English. He summarized the Pennsylvania and Auburn systems, favoring the former and describing the architecture of Cherry Hill; he also presented plans for a small district prison to be built on a radial design. In 1847 the first of the new Swedish prisons was erected, and in 1878 a central prison at Långholmen, near Stockholm, was constructed on a plan similar to Haviland's New Jersey State Prison at Trenton.

In the Austro-Hungarian Empire new prison construction closely followed German models. Institutions at Graz (1869–72) and Stein (1870–73) consisted of three radiating cell wings and an administrative wing. Plzeň (1874–78) in Bohemia was most similar to Cherry Hill; it had seven cell wings radiating from a central inspection rotunda with an eighth wing for administrative offices facing the front.

V CRUCIBLE OF GOOD INTENTIONS

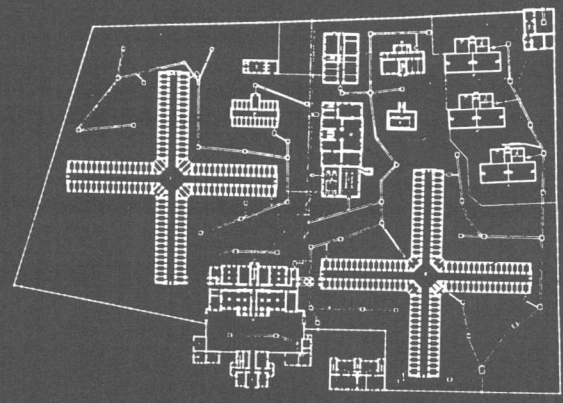

Russia St. Petersburg
Kresty
1884–90

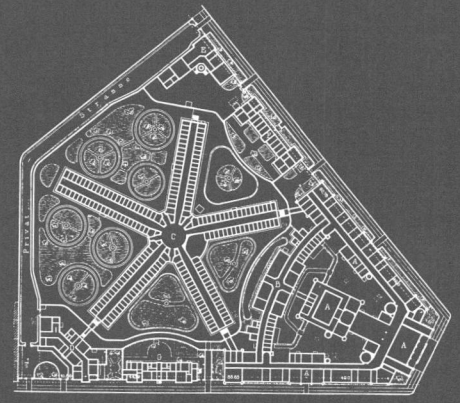

Germany Berlin
Moabit II
1869–79

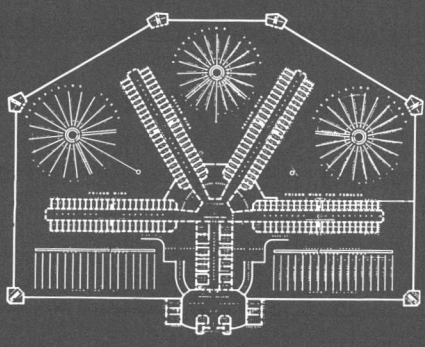

England London
Pentonville
1840–42

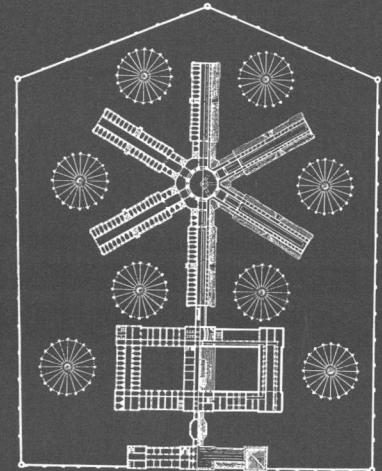

Italy Milan
San Vittore
1867–79

Cherry Hill

Model for the World

Cherry Hill: Model for the World

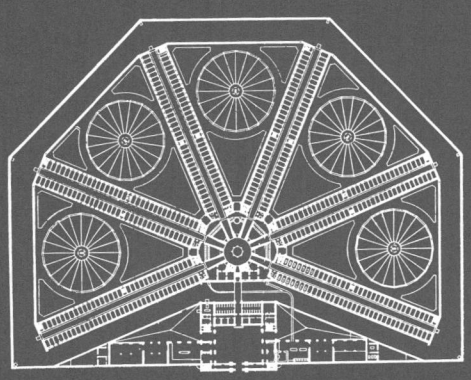

France Paris
Mazas
1843–50

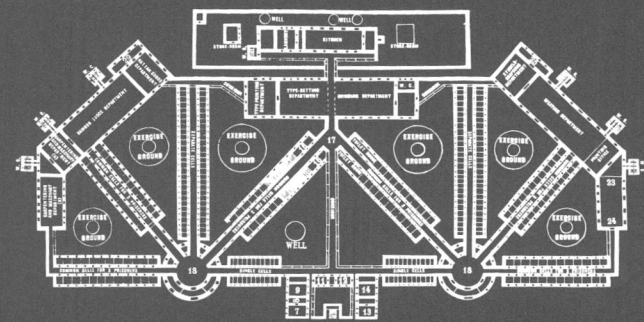

China Beijing
First Prison
1909–12

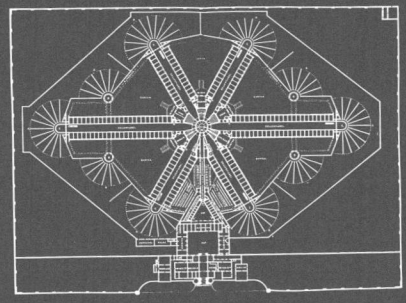

Belgium Louvain
1856–60

Worldwide variations on Haviland's plans. The impact of his designs for Cherry Hill, as Eastern State Penitentiary was commonly known, and the New Jersey State Prison in Trenton was both immediate and long-lived. The radial plan could accommodate a variety of arrangements and numbers of cell wings while retaining the advantage of surveillance from a central rotunda. Three hundred prisons throughout the world can trace their paternity to Cherry Hill.

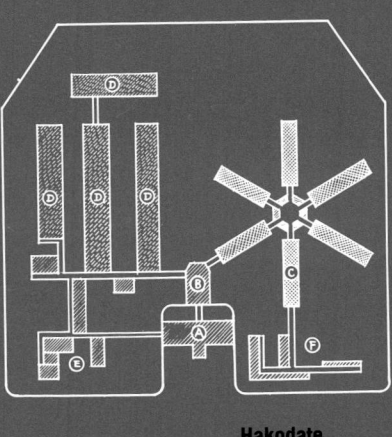

Japan Hakodate
1931

(Not to scale)

V Crucible of Good Intentions

Attributed to William Langenheim (1807–1874) and Frederick Langenheim (1809–1879), *Rotunda at Eastern State Penitentiary*, c. 1855. Salted-paper print, diameter 6¾". George Eastman House, Rochester, New York.

Rotunda of Kiangsu First Prison, China, c. 1910, based on the original rotunda at Eastern State Penitentiary.

Latin American Reforms

The countries of Latin America, with one or two exceptions, built few large central prisons until recently. The earlier structures, usually erected in or near capitals, were almost always radial, reflecting direct North American or European, particularly French, influences. Brazil led the way, constructing a house of correction in Rio de Janeiro in 1837. There is some indication that the Brazilian government had received plans of Cherry Hill and had fully intended to build a prison on Haviland's designs but, for unknown reasons, built a prison based instead on earlier British radial models.[12] In 1853 the Brazilian government sent officials to Philadelphia, Trenton, and other prison sites in the United States; nevertheless, they built only one other radial prison, in Recife in 1855.

In 1853 Peru sent a representative, Mariano Paz Soldán, to the United States to evaluate prison systems and their architecture. He was very much impressed with Haviland's Eastern State Penitentiary and remained a corresponding member of the Pennsylvania Prison Society. Paz Soldán was later responsible for building in Lima the country's first reform penitentiary, a multiwing radial prison with a large central rotunda, and he served as its first warden.

Argentina demonstrated the most enthusiasm among Latin American countries for building new prisons based on the Pennsylvania plan. The national penitentiary in Buenos Aires by Ernesto Bunge was the first such one erected, in 1872, and other prisons were built on the Haviland radial plan as far south as Tierra del Fuego. A large six-wing radial prison opened in 1939 near the capital.

Other Haviland-inspired prisons were constructed in Bogota, Colombia (1876), Quito, Ecuador (1870s), and Mexico City (1885–1900). The prison in Mexico City was designed by Antonio Torres Torija and consisted of seven radiating wings with a large observation tower in the center.

East Asian Modernization

One of the first effects of Westernization in Japan was a new concern with prison conditions; changes in the medieval prisons of the country began with the advent of the Meiji period of reform in 1868. Shikueya Ohara, a jurist and underdirector of the prison administration, visited British colonial prisons and sent officials to the United States and Europe. The result was the enthusiastic adoption of the use of solitary confinement and the acceptance of the radial prison plan as official policies. The first of the new prisons, Miyagi (1879), said to be designed by an English architect, consisted of six wings arranged very much like Louvain prison in Belgium.[13] Over thirty-six radial prisons were built in Japan, the most common plan featuring a series of fanlike arrays based on the Trenton or Pentonville plan, as in Tokyo (1879), or occasionally five-or six-wing, full-circle designs, as at Gifu and Hakodate, which opened in 1931. At Kagoshima (1908), the typical radial prison also employed gothic-inspired details for the entrance gate, a gesture wholly independent of local architectural traditions. More purely radial prisons were erected in Japan than in any other country except Spain, and only Belgium has rivaled Japan in the consistency of the architecture.[14]

Prison reform came later to China, although the nineteenth century brought increasing familiarity with Western ideas and institutions. Representatives were sent to international conferences on penology, notably those at Frankfurt, Germany, in 1846, and Washington, D.C., in 1910. Conditions in nineteenth-century Chinese jails were much like those John Howard had encountered in Europe a century earlier. Foreign visitors, even in the early twentieth century, reported the confinement of prisoners in wooden cages, sometimes with as many as twenty in a single cage. Improvements were initiated, it has been suggested, to demonstrate their advanced thinking to critics in the West.[15] Although representatives made trips to Europe and America under government auspices, it was Western ideas taken to China by Japanese legal scholars and architects that had the most influence on reform there. The first of the new prisons was opened in Hubei in 1906, and by 1918 the entire prison system had been rebuilt, resulting in about forty model prisons. Almost all of these were constructed on some variation of a radial design with a combination of solitary and congregate cells. Some of the plans were complicated, such as that of the Beijing First Prison (1909–12), consisting of repeated five-wing structures reminiscent of the Trenton layout. This prison is still in use, although as many as ten prisoners now sleep in a single cell. The central rotundas in the Beijing First Prison, as in many others in China, bear a striking resemblance to Haviland's rotunda at Cherry Hill, with a balcony on the second level that allows a view of the single-story buildings and the exercise areas.

From even this abbreviated review of world prison construction following the completion of Eastern State Penitentiary, it is clear that Haviland's innovative architecture was the most potent vehicle for the diffusion of the Pennsylvania system. The social experiment of solitary confinement in cells and the radial plan that gave it a workable, signature form were integrated in prototype prisons in London, Berlin, Paris, St. Petersburg, and Madrid. With modifications, these institutions spread the influence to provinces, colonies, and developing nations still farther afield. About three hundred prisons worldwide can trace their paternity to Cherry Hill.[16] Its influence was strongly manifest everywhere in the world, except in the United States.

The iron middle gate added to the entrance in 1924–25. From *Annual Report*, 1926.

Accommodation and Redefinition in the Twentieth Century

JEFFREY A. COHEN

Shortly after the penitentiary passed a century of service, a new outer gateway was added to the prison's main facade.[1] Placed abruptly in front of the original south portal, the addition interrupted the severe gothic forms of the prison's most representational face, announcing that its heroic ordering of large, sharply squared and molded stones and its rhetoric embodied in historical allusion were outdated and superfluous. The roughly laid stonework was closest in treatment to the low retaining wall of the terrace, the front's least monumental element. Only the gateway's flat, keystoned arches gestured beyond the prosaic. The arches —implausibly wide and shallow, supported by hidden steel lintels—betrayed a gap between older intentions and the expediency of later practices. The commonplace form of the added gate spoke of lowered confidence in the institution's founding ideals, of diminished expectations from the prison and of diminished resources devoted to it.

Eastern State Penitentiary was no longer a monument to the promise of rehabilitation. It had become a fatalistic part of the correctional bureaucracy, a

The new front gateway, erected in 1937–38, with the original entrance behind. From *The Philadelphia Inquirer*, April 1945.

VI Crucible of Good Intentions

warehouse for the state's toughest convicts. Little of the founders' optimism about human nature or the philanthropic tenor of its original governance survived. The penitentiary was viewed as a place of unpleasant necessity, where the focus was on firm discipline, if occasionally leavened with personal acts of humanity.

The penitentiary's last seven decades were marked by heated debates about its nature and its future. In 1913 the pretense that the state was adhering to the old Pennsylvania system of separate confinement was abandoned, long after it had ceased to exist in fact for much of Cherry Hill's population. From that decade on, there were repeated calls for the demolition or reassignment of the facility. The two most important turning points came in 1928, when the first buildings of a new Eastern State Penitentiary opened at Graterford, thirty-five miles northwest of Philadelphia, and in 1954, when the state redefined part of the older facility of Cherry Hill as a diagnostic center. At both times state authorities chose to retain a building complex recognized as irredeemably obsolete and restrictive.

The press focused public awareness on the prison's uncertain future and on episodes of disorder and danger—on notorious criminals, escapes, riots, scandals, murders, and suicides. The penitentiary's immediate neighbors recall some positive aspects—of the prison as employer and provider of modest services and goods—but they also probably had a more intimate sense of the numbing sameness and the imminence of force that reigned within. Since the 1940s the historical significance of the prison has been brought increasingly to scholarly, governmental, and popular attention. In 1971 Cherry Hill was finally closed, and the future of this landmark has been uncertain ever since.

At the beginning of the twentieth century, Eastern State Penitentiary was an orderly and still proud institution, but one crippled by the twin afflictions under which it had struggled for decades: overcrowding and a stultifying restriction on prison labor. On the last day of the last century there were 1,175 inmates in 760 cells;[2] more than half of the prisoners were sharing cells, as had significant portions of the

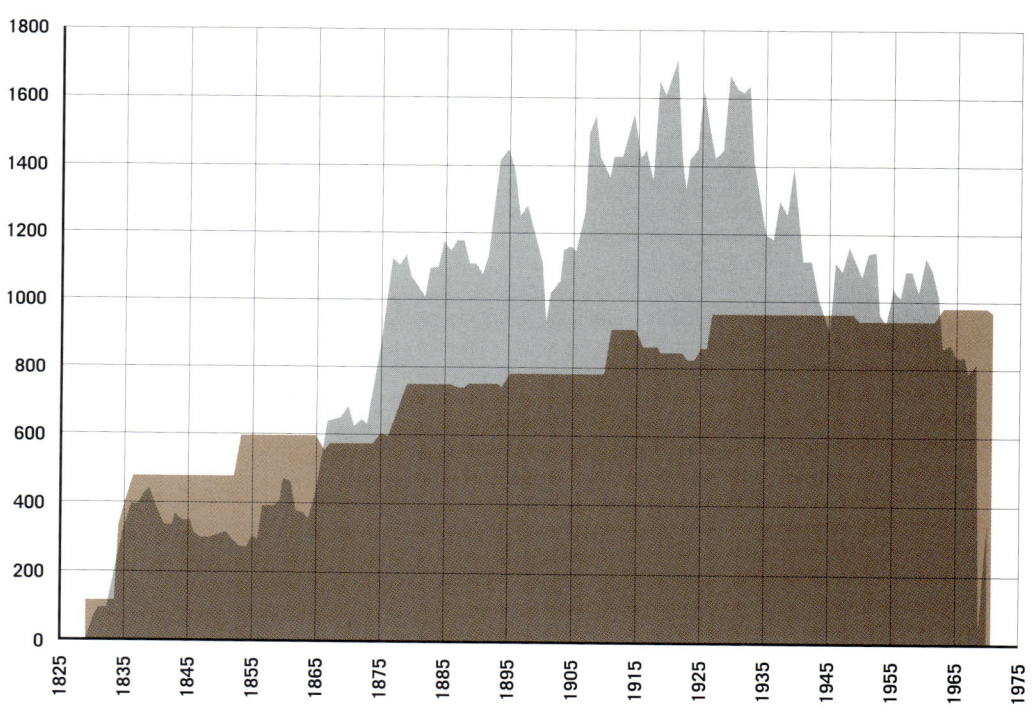

Chart showing the prison population and the number of cells at Eastern State Penitentiary from 1829 to 1971. By Marianna Thomas Architects.

Inmate population.

Number of cells.

Southeast face of cellblock three, the hospital block, altered in 1900 to provide tall, arched openings for special cells and a separate yard for consumptives. From *Annual Report*, 1905.

prison population since the late 1860s. Their programmatic intent hobbled by an overcrowded condition beyond their control, Cherry Hill authorities rationalized at the turn of the century that separate confinement was unnecessary for those incapable of reform, although it was suitable for "accidental criminals" and first offenders.[3] The Pennsylvania system, redefined as "individual treatment," persisted mainly in this limited amount of separation, opposition to congregate or mechanized labor, and the continuing practices of dining in cells and frequent visitation by officials and religious instructors, but a stream of accommodations had built up over the previous decades, relaxing the old strictures.

The prison-labor problem had also grown more serious in the late nineteenth century. Free and organized labor had decried the competition from a captive work force and in 1883 succeeded in having a law passed that required Pennsylvania prison manufactures to be stamped "convict made," with the name of the institution. New York restricted the entry of such goods, closing an important market. But the most severe measure came in 1897, when Pennsylvania passed the Muehlbronner Act, which stipulated that no more than 10 percent of a prison's inmates could produce goods for outside consumption.[4] The idleness that resulted aggravated the monotony of confinement, and the reduction of income made the prison more expensive to run. For decades to follow the prison administration would have to contrive other ways of employing prisoners productively, using inmate labor for building and maintenance of the prison, for work in the repair and "hobby" shops—whose products were marketed to the prison's neighbors—and for the manufacture of goods sold within state and institutional networks. Yet, even these measures left many prisoners idle. Despite the repeated protests of the prison's trustees, the restriction on labor persisted through the mid-1920s.

The prison entered the new century without two of its most devoted champions. Richard Vaux (whose father Roberts Vaux was an early proponent of the prison) had been an inspector since 1842 and the penitentiary's leading advocate for half a century when he died in 1895. Warden Michael Cassidy, an irrepressible spokesman among prison professionals, died in 1900, after nearly forty years in the service of Cherry Hill.[5] The deaths of these two ardent supporters of the Pennsylvania system broke an extraordinary continuity of commitment that reached back to the prison's founders.

By the time the institution lost Cassidy it had acquired a new nemesis, tuberculosis, called the "convict's friend." This disease accounted for the majority of prison deaths from the mid-1890s to about 1920, claiming ten or more prisoners each year. There were also outbreaks of smallpox and typhoid, and medical conditions became an urgent concern.[6]

Harrisburg Intervenes

After decades of largely local initiative and control, the government of Pennsylvania began to fill the vacuum left by the deaths of Vaux and Cassidy, and to respond to the problems emerging at Cherry Hill. The most notable effect was an extensive renovation of the prison in the first years of the new century, motivated in part by

VI CRUCIBLE OF GOOD INTENTIONS

Shop building, erected in 1905–7 east of cellblock four, to accommodate carpentry, pipe, and blacksmith shops. The round smokestack of the power plant rises behind. From *Annual Report*, 1909.

health issues, but dedicated also to a general modernization of the facility. Architect William S. Vaux, Jr., surveyed the entire site in April 1900, and with his partner, George S. Morris, devised plans for a number of new buildings that were constructed over the next eight years. In 1901 a new boiler and engine house with an enormous chimney stack (demolished in the 1950s) was completed between blocks three and four to provide heat and light for the entire prison. A few years later, a storehouse addition was built to the northwest of the existing kitchen and gristmill building, between blocks four and five, and an industrial building was constructed between blocks five and six in 1905–7 "to house goods and operate various portions of manufacturing departments" (it was later used as a laundry and chapel-auditorium).[7] A shop building (also demolished in the 1950s) north of the new boiler was added in the same years to house carpentry, blacksmith, and pipe shops. And a new emergency hospital (demolished in 1937) for contagious diseases was added in 1907–8 between blocks two and three. With their rusticated granite walls and grouped industrial windows, these new buildings presented themselves as modern, solid, and utilitarian, but they also offered a characterizing overlay of gothic detail—more than any other buildings within the walls—that modestly reinvoked the rhetoric of higher purposes. This building campaign also included major improvements to water, heating, electrical, and drainage systems, and general renovations to the cellblocks and the grounds. The hospital facilities in block three were provided with a new operating room, a new skylit ward with sixteen beds, and well-ventilated ground-story cells with open yards for tubercular inmates. Most of the construction was done by prisoners, as had been the usual practice since Warden Cassidy's new blocks—eight, nine, and ten—were begun three decades earlier.[8]

The use of inmate labor on the new buildings reflected the fact that solitary work was already being replaced by group efforts in workshops and in the daily operation of the prison. An investigative report in 1902 criticized the use of inmates as household servants for the warden and his staff. The following year prison inspectors noted that as many as 200 inmates were aimlessly roaming the corridors.[9] In 1903 the wearing of hoods outside the cells was officially made optional. Such erosion of the pure form of the Pennsylvania system troubled its champions, who publicly and repeatedly protested the inadequate accommodations and increasingly limited opportunities for productive employment.[10] Nonetheless, authorities at Eastern State Penitentiary saw validity in what remained of the system and defended it against the partisans of congregate prisons.[11] They continued to emphasize the widespread adoption of their system in Europe and noted that staffing costs were lower than those of congregate prisons. But they could not deny that the income from prison industries at Cherry Hill rarely matched that earned at congregate prisons. In response, Cherry Hill's advocates repeatedly underscored the preeminence of the rehabilitative value of work over the pursuit of profits.

The inspectors' appeals finally convinced the state legislature of the need for additional separate cells, particularly for first offenders, who were felt to be most at risk from association. The state funded block twelve, with 120 cells, which was

Accommodation and Redefinition in the Twentieth Century

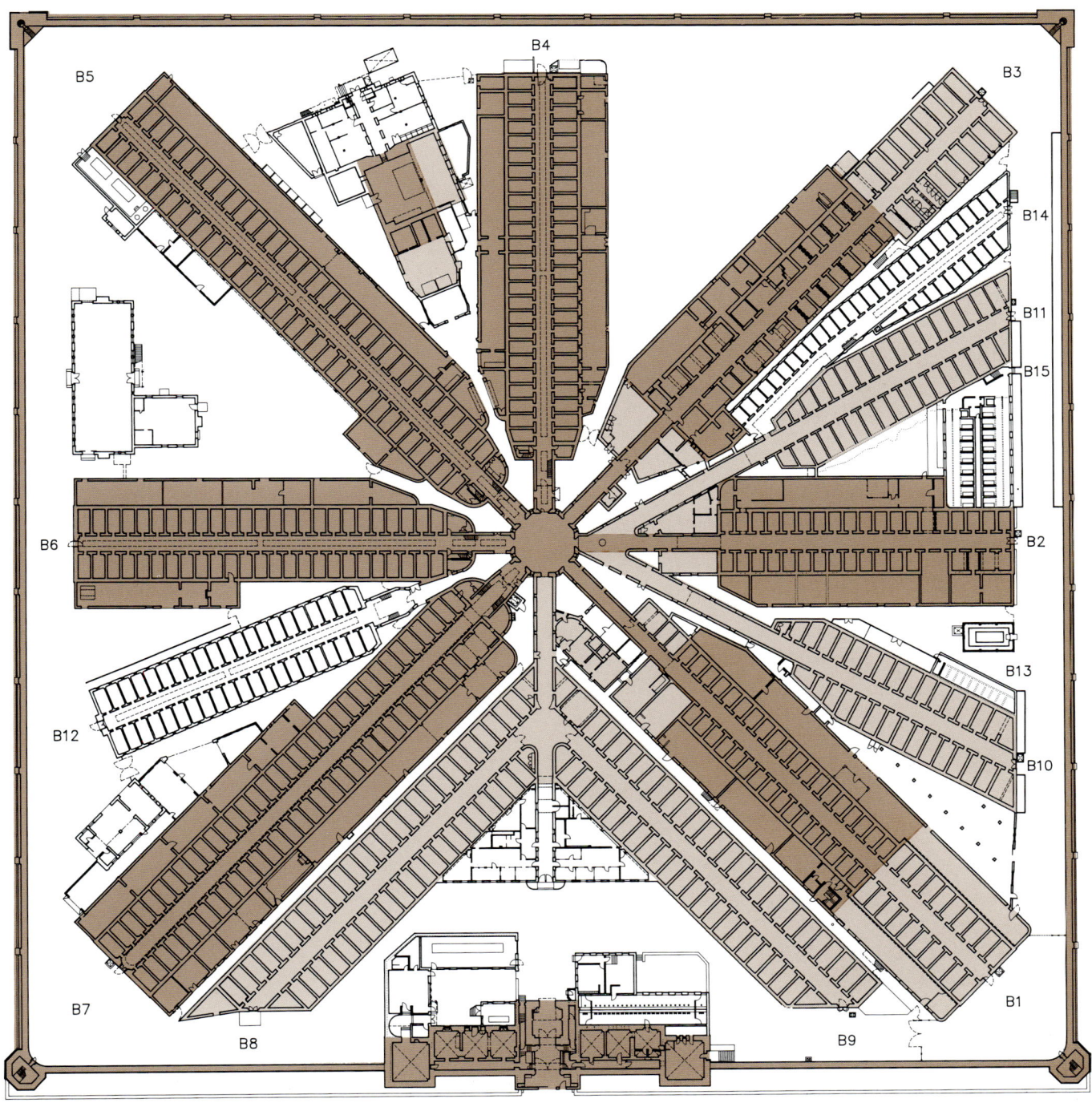

Plan of the existing structures at Eastern State Penitentiary, showing the features that survive in 1993 from the initial construction of 1822–36 (in dark brown) and the features added before 1900 (in light brown). By Marianna Thomas Architects. Historic conditions have been taken from Frédéric-Auguste Demetz and Guillaume-Abel Blouet, Rapports sur les pénitenciers des Etats-Unis *(Paris: Imprimerie royale, 1837),* and from a survey by William S. Vaux, Jr., 1900, at the Historical Society of Pennsylvania.

Features surviving from the initial construction of 1822–36.

Surviving features added before 1900.

Unshaded features postdate 1900.

Cellblock twelve, erected in 1909–11 between cellblocks six and seven. From *Annual Report*, 1912.

Interior of cellblock twelve. From *Annual Report*, 1912.

built by prisoners in 1909–11.[12] Like the garage building put up at the same time, it was constructed of reinforced concrete, which gave the new building a brighter, cleaner appearance than its older neighbors, although the new block's three tiers of identical openings presented a cold and mechanistic countenance for a system of "individual treatment."

These physical improvements were accompanied by modifications in discipline and methods. Illiterate prisoners were taught to read, and trade schools were set up in roofed-over yards, in which inmates produced "useful and artistic" articles for sale.[13] In the annual report for 1912, the inspectors proclaimed that "we have virtually a new Institution, on the basis of the separate system as it was originally devised, so that the life and methods of today have practically but little similarity or relationship to those of years past."[14]

The Board of Public Charities, which oversaw the operation of the prison on the state's behalf, meanwhile took a different tack. Although it commended the physical condition and management of Cherry Hill, despite its overcrowding (the board was more critical of its Pittsburgh counterpart), from 1908 it advised repeatedly that both facilities should relocate to large rural tracts. Seven years later, such an act was passed. It directed that Cherry Hill be abandoned, and that the two penitentiaries be combined at a new institution, under one management, in Centre County.[15] But relocation was quickly aborted. The proposed site for the new prison in the middle of the state, far from the two populated ends and therefore burdensome for the transportation of prisoners and visitors, kept the measure from execution.

Another proposal by the Board of Public Charities appears to have had more immediate effect. The board's advice that the "antiquated" laws governing these institutions be "brought up to date" may have influenced Governor John K. Tener, in January 1913, to recommend congregate "worship, labor, learning, and recreation."[16] The result was a bill that passed in July

Accommodation and Redefinition in the Twentieth Century

The chapel, opened in 1914 on the second story of the industrial building, between cellblocks five and six. From *Annual Report*, 1925.

The library on the upper story of the central rotunda, containing more than ten thousand volumes. From *Annual Report*, 1925.

VI Crucible of Good Intentions

Prisoners constructing the third floor of cellblock fourteen in 1926. From *Annual Report*, 1926.

of that year stipulating that "the proper authorities of the Eastern State Penitentiary are authorized, at their discretion, to have any or all of the persons confined in the said penitentiary congregated" for these purposes.[17] The new law mandated less than it allowed and may simply have ratified some measures already in operation at Cherry Hill, but it soon translated into a wider range of congregate activities. For some of the inspectors, this may have meant publicly acknowledging the end of a long-held ideal. They barely acknowledged the law in their annual reports. Evidence of change came quietly, without rhetoric proclaiming a new mission or system. The inspectors announced in early 1914 that "new methods, together with new ideas and standards which have come into vogue in the last few years, have transformed the old life of our Institution."[18] In 1915 it was noted that on April 5 of the previous year, "the prisoners were for the first time in the history of the Institution allowed outside their cells for the purpose of religious worship."[19] This took place in the industrial building, where the large second-story space was fitted up for this purpose. Similar measures soon affected dining, work, and recreation for most of the prison population.

Still, the restriction on labor was felt severely; according to the president of the Board of Public Charities:

The law in this State covering the employment of prisoners in jails states that it must be limited to one-tenth the total number of inmates. This law is the result of labor unions and is not only unfair, but inhuman. . . . Lack of facilities for their employment and the law, as stated above, in most cases, produces, especially where the prisoner is serving a long term sentence, a distress in mind and body.[20]

Remedy for this situation was sought, and in 1915 the state's Prison Labor Commission was established to oversee production of goods to supply other state institutions. Within a few years the commission founded shops for the manufacture of shoes and hosiery. In 1918 Prison Labor Commission shops employed 107 inmates, while 345 more worked indoors and out in activities such as building maintenance or cooking. Another 77 inmates were listed as sick, leaving 839 idle, over 60 percent of the entire population of 1,371 inmates. That year the commission started to install power-driven machinery, and soon additional cell yards were combined and covered to provide work space. In April 1925 the state finally overturned the 1897 Muehlbronner Act, legalizing what was called the "public account system"; the following year 1,079 of the 1,487 inmates found some form of employment in the institution.[21]

The state also made sweeping administrative changes in these years, disbanding the Board of Public Charities and the Prison Labor Commission in May 1921.[22] Prison issues were to be handled by the Bureau of Restoration in the Department of Welfare. The penitentiary's old Board of Inspectors was replaced by a Board of Trustees, and the boards' long run of detailed annual reports soon came to an end. In the 1930s the only official records of the prison to be published were brief sections of the biennial reports of the Department of Welfare, closing a long chapter of proud and public advocacy.

The idea of relocating the prison to the country, proposed repeatedly for its

Accommodation and Redefinition in the Twentieth Century

Power machinery in the weaving shop, built in the 1920s in the combined spaces of former cell yards. From *Annual Report*, 1925.

promise of more healthful surroundings, ample space for recreation, and the prospect of agricultural work, resurfaced in 1924. The prison's Board of Trustees proposed a large, new prison, offering employment in farming, reforestation, and healthful outdoor activities, on a 2,000-acre site within thirty-five miles of Philadelphia.[23] The legislature complied in May 1925, authorizing the purchase of land at Graterford, in Montgomery County. The new facility was built using prisoners bused from Cherry Hill and later housed in temporary barracks at Graterford. By 1930 about 800 inmates had moved into the first completed cellblock.[24] That number increased to about 1,800 within a few years, allowing the inmate population at Cherry Hill to drop from a high of 1,696 in 1922 to 1,269 in 1933 and 1,174 in 1936. Graterford would function for decades as the "farm branch" of Eastern State Penitentiary, under the same warden.[25]

Twentieth-Century Life at Cherry Hill

The construction of the new prison at Graterford led many to expect that Cherry Hill would be abandoned in a few years,[26] but, in fact, the state continued to fund improvements to the older complex. In April 1926 the trustees approved the construction of a new cellblock with 117 cells on three stories. Construction began immediately, and block fourteen, built of reinforced concrete by prison labor, was completed the following April at a cost of $56,324. Bent into the tight sliver between block eleven and the hospital (block three), the new building was meant to segregate younger prisoners, protecting them from association with the rest of the prison population.[27] It brought the total number of cells to nearly 950.

After the removal of legal strictures on congregation in 1913, the penitentiary discovered a new normality in routines that assembled inmates for dining, worship, labor, education, and recreation. Workshops replaced more of the cell yards, particularly after 1925, when the annual report proudly displayed photographs of new, mechanized facilities for shoemaking, weaving, and printing. A fresh emphasis was placed on recreational programs: physical exercise was now "recognized as of prime importance to health," the annual report for 1920 pronounced, and "uplifting amusement is appreciated as magic medicine."[28] A Pennsylvania law of June 1923 stipulated that prisoners be allowed two hours of outdoor exercise daily, weather permitting.[29] Inmates practiced calisthenics in their cells and other activities in the daily "yard out." Sports was the main topic of a weekly prison newspaper, *The Umpire*; one surviving issue from 1913 recorded

VI Crucible of Good Intentions

Interior of one of the two dining halls adapted from former exercise yards in 1924. Tablecloths were provided on Sundays and holidays, and the holiday decorations were described as a "morale building factor."

the score of a football game pitting a "white" team against "light blacks."[30]

Other important changes irrevocably altered everyday life for the staff and inmates. In July 1924 the yards of cellblocks four and five, adjoining the kitchen, were transformed into two narrow dining halls that together seated nearly 800 inmates. And in 1923 all female prisoners were relocated from their long-time quarters in block two to a campus of small cottages at the new State Industrial Home for Women at Muncy.[31] This array of changes transformed the internal culture of Cherry Hill, engendering new social mechanisms and the testing of new limits.

By 1916 the prisoners had established the Honor and Friendship Club to help families and dischargees and to arrange burials or entertainment. The following year the club began showing movies provided by Monarch Film Company, and under club auspices, prisoners rolled bandages for the Red Cross.[32] Within two years, however, the club was embroiled in scandal; "agitators" reportedly took it over, and finding a sympathetic new inspector, W. A. Dunlap, and moral instructor, Rev. Joseph Welch, they filed complaints about their treatment under the administration of Robert J. McKenty, who had been warden since 1909. An investigating committee of the Board of Public Charities conducted hearings, dismissed Dunlap and Welch, discontinued the club, and recommended that Warden McKenty establish firmer control.[33]

The McKenty administration, recalled as idealistic in the 1930s, was riddled with problems, some exacerbated by the loss of experienced officers to the military in World War I.[34] A "wild" breakout was attempted in 1922, spurred by drug use. And a cabal of prisoners known as "the four horsemen" reportedly dominated the prison—selling jobs, sex, and favors. Inmates charged that murder victims were certified as having died of natural causes. A grand jury investigated, and McKenty was fired in 1923, succeeded by the firm disciplinarian John C. Groome. He retired after five years, but much the same tenor of administration was followed by his successor, Herbert E. Smith.[35]

Several escape attempts bedeviled Groome, just as they would plague Smith in the decades to follow. In July 1923 six prisoners armed with pistols held up unarmed guards and used a ladder to climb over the east wall. One prisoner was soon apprehended in Honolulu, and another, number C566, Leo Callahan, was never recaptured. In November four inmates attempted to escape via the main gate, one successfully.[36]

The new warden responded with sweeping changes in the guard staff, replacing many with military veterans. Sentry boxes were built on the corner towers, now provided with powerful Krag repeating rifles and Thompson submachine guns; iron gates were placed at the inner ends of the cellblock corridors. A new intermediate iron gate was added to the two in the front portal. The warden's offices, for decades located off the main corridor, between blocks one and nine, were returned to the front building, more insulated from inmate eyes and ears. Visiting rooms for outsiders, formerly special cells within each block, were consolidated in a single space in the east basement of the front building, where a barrier between inmate and visitor prevented the passing of contraband.[37]

A grand jury investigation in 1924 revealed that the main disciplinary measure was confinement to the "Klondike" on the gallery of cellblock four, with the skylight covered over and the interior painted black.[38] The prisoner would be placed, without clothes, in the damp, dark, unfurnished cell and given only bread and water. The report also criticized Smith, the future warden, for arranging mismatched pairs of prisoners to box as a means of punishment.[39] And it was probably in the early to mid-1920s that cellblock thirteen, a range of ten small cells for more serious administrative segregation, was added to the north side of the end of block ten.

Even after security was tightened, escape attempts were frequent. Just after New Year's Day of 1925, James Gordon hid in a truckload of hot ashes and successfully made his way out. Convicts also tried to scale the walls or crawl through the sewers, but more common were attempts to escape by digging tunnels. Tunneling efforts were foiled in April 1924 and June 1926, after which concrete floors were poured in those cells that still had wood planking. Warden Smith estimated that about thirty tunnels were dug in the late 1930s when there was a shortage of guards; excavations for a new central heating system in 1939 uncovered many aborted underground passages. The most notorious tunnel escape from Cherry Hill occurred in April 1945, involving twenty-two men, ten of whom never made it out of the prison. Most of those who escaped, including Clarence Klinedinst, "Botchie" Van Sant, and Willie Sutton, were caught that same day, and the rest within two months.

There were other forms of prison disorder: a hunger strike and riot in August–September 1933 (precipitating some reforms); a mass break for the wall in November 1933 (the ladder broke); a fire set in June 1940; a riot over war rationing in March 1942; a dynamite plot in December 1944; and another hunger strike in October 1945 over the extended time in punishment blocks given the recaptured escapees from the previous April's break.[40]

The pressure at Cherry Hill was eased somewhat by the expansion of Graterford to a capacity of nearly 2,000 inmates. From the 1930s to the 1960s, the population at Cherry Hill ranged between about 900 and 1,400 inmates in roughly 950 cells. But the total population in the two institutions had doubled in the decade since the mid-1920s, topping 3,000 inmates. The effects of the persistent national depression during these

View of the main entrance, from the southwest. From *Annual Report*, 1925.

VI   Crucible of Good Intentions

years were undoubtedly reflected in these numbers, and in 1934 it was reported that the average age of offenders had dropped from 32 to 25. The economic crisis hindered parole; in 1933, there were 94 otherwise qualified prisoners who were unable to secure the necessary promise of employment. Three years later the release of 74 more was prevented for the same reason.[41]

In the reorganized scheme of operations from the late 1920s, Cherry Hill was designated a maximum-security facility (Graterford was medium-security) meant for chronic recidivists and others for whom rehabilitation was not deemed likely. It was also to serve as the receiving prison for the eastern part of the state; following a 1934 initiative, new inmates would be observed for thirty days, classified, and often sent to a more appropriate institution. The classification function notwithstanding, the emphasis at Cherry Hill was on maintaining discipline, particularly under "Hardboiled" or "Hardball" Smith (whose tenure ended with the repercussions of the Klinedinst-Sutton escape in 1945). In 1938 Smith testified that any attempt at rehabilitation at Eastern State Penitentiary was "a joke.... We can't even maintain discipline satisfactorily." One-third of the men were "insane," "defectives," or "degenerate," he claimed, and overcrowding made reform efforts particularly difficult.[42]

Details of life at Cherry Hill before the end of World War II emerge from the recollections of former inmates and staff.[43] After women left cellblock two, which was known to have somewhat better accommodations, bribes could reportedly procure a cell there. It was known as "old farts' alley." The institution was largely segregated. In the late 1940s African Americans—whose numbers rose from less than a third of the population before the war to more than half in 1948—were housed in cellblock four and the ground floor of cellblock five; both adjoined the kitchen, where the inmate staff was disproportionately black. Cellblocks seven and twelve were entirely white and cellblocks eight and nine were predominantly so. Other parts were more mixed, particularly the three punishment blocks: the gallery of block five, block one—where prisoners ate in their cells and were denied yard time or other recreations—and the most severe, block thirteen. Block fourteen was the quarantine, for newcomers and young offenders. Nearly every block had its own barbershop and shower room and a range of shops that in some cases determined who was placed there.[44]

Work at Eastern State Penitentiary was more varied and sometimes more remunerative for the inmates than at other prisons. Shops conducted by the Department of Welfare produced clothing and shoes, and did printing for other state institutions. Many inmates were employed by the penitentiary in maintenance, service, car repair, rag shops, and a variety of other tasks. In the hobby shops, prisoners built toys and models, particularly of ships; during World War II they made models for the identification of aircraft and ships by defense personnel.[45] The war also saw a notorious episode of "convict capitalists," who contracted with the Marine Corps to make hundreds of thousands of tent pegs, employed their fellow prisoners, and profited handsomely.[46] The war elicited extraordinary voluntary responses from convicts at Cherry Hill: men earning between 10 and 40 cents per day subscribed for $50,000 in war bonds in the first ten months of the war. They worked extra hours for the War Production Board. They donated blood for transfusions and skin for grafts.[47]

The prison offered training in trades and general educational classes. During the two-hour "yard out" each afternoon, inmates mingled outdoors and played organized sports. Baseball, football, quoits, and other games were contrived to suit the grounds, using painted lines that survive on some of the perimeter walls. Balls were often knocked over the walls—4,300 homemade baseballs during a twelve-month period in 1933–34—and their return from outside was suspected as a means of smuggling in drugs. Football was a particularly serious matter. Photographs from the 1930s show inmates wearing full pads and uniforms (emblazoned with a large P), visiting coaches giving advice, and an annual game against Graterford (always an away game). But in an era that placed such emphasis on sports, the prison's spatial constraints were a constant frustration. A tragic extreme was the case of footballer Frank Pisano, aged 26, who died in October 1939 after smashing headlong into a wall. From the 1930s, obsolete secondary buildings were demolished in order to clear the grounds and allow larger recreation areas.[48]

The serving of meals, run in two shifts each, marked the intervals between morning work and afternoon yard time. Food was recognized as a powerful encouragement to compliance, and there was little compunction at denying it to preserve order; in September 1934 the warden withheld the third meal of the day until the spirit of "open rebellion" among the prisoners improved.[49] Movies were frequently shown upstairs in the industrial building, and inmates had access to a ten-thousand-volume library that was relocated from the upper story of the central hub to a covered yard off cellblock two. For a long time prisoners had personalized their cells at Cherry Hill with painted decorations; in 1941 art classes were held and that year prisoners' paintings were exhibited at a center-city department store. Musical activities of various sorts were popular, and concerts by prisoners were broadcast on local radio stations.[50]

Despite these recreational and educational activities, the prison was a dangerous and, at times, a violent place. From year to year newspaper reports of murders and suicides publicized only the most serious incidents.[51] Charges of brutality by guards emerged in the early

1930s, prompting investigations and calls for better training of prison personnel.[52] A guard was killed in 1944, and shortly after the war the prison's notorious "goon squad"—guards stationed in the center hub to respond quickly with force to any threat of disorder in the cellblocks—began its reign.[53] There were ballgames and films and crafts at Cherry Hill, but it was no summer camp.

A Last Modernization

Over the decades Eastern State Penitentiary had several times been called obsolete, but in testimony from early 1933 the tone was more adamant and its source more official. "We cannot reform men when we place them in dark and unhealthful cells, in an environment worse than the one from which they came," Warden Smith stated. "All principles of modern penology are opposed to conditions which exist here."[54] Smith was no great champion of modern penology, and he may have said this partially to excuse the lack of treatment programs at Cherry Hill, but his point was well taken. The urban location was considered inappropriate for a maximum-security prison, and the crowded grounds made recreation difficult; the assembly hall could accommodate only one-third of the population at a time, the dining halls only half. The workshops lining the long flanks of each block cut off ventilation and concentrated heat and noise at "intolerable" levels. And it was estimated that hundreds of thousands of dollars in staff and maintenance costs could be saved by consolidating the two institutions at Graterford.[55]

Such charges notwithstanding, there was no consolidation, only relatively modest changes in the architectural fabric over the next decades: in the late 1930s the new front portal and a new storage building (outside the northwest corner of the perimeter wall) were constructed; in the 1940s the front angle between blocks eight and nine was filled in with additional rooms used for classification of inmates and administration of the parole program.[56] There was some relief from overcrowding during World War II: according to a 1944 report, the population fell by a few hundred to approach 1,000 prisoners, not many more than the 945 "usable" cells.[57]

Demolition of the engine house in the early 1950s, to make way for an athletic field between cellblocks three and four.

VI Crucible of Good Intentions

At this time a new, more authoritative charge of obsolescence was leveled at the prison by criminologists Harry Elmer Barnes, Negley K. Teeters, and Albert G. Fraser. They were unequivocal in their views: Eastern State Penitentiary was "hopelessly antiquated." Coats of whitewash could not conceal "the flavor of antiquity and obsolescence which pervades the institution." Discipline was difficult to maintain. "Eastern Penitentiary," they concluded, "is one of the worst prisons in any civilized state.... To pour any more money into this plant, in the effort to renovate or extend it, would be quasi-criminal folly."[58] Governor Edward Martin echoed their comments in July 1944, calling Eastern State Penitentiary "not fit for human habitation."

Closing the Philadelphia facility would be given top priority, he averred, in an effort to give Pennsylvania once again "the best and most modern penal system in the country."[59]

Barnes and his colleagues offered some influential suggestions about the state's administration of its prisons. Under the Department of Welfare, the Bureau of Correction had not fared well. Hospitals and charitable institutions received most of the funds and attention, a point demonstrated by the thin sections devoted to prisons in the department's annual reports. It was time, therefore, to elevate corrections to departmental status.[60] In April 1945 the legislature adopted the recommendations of a gubernatorial committee and authorized the abandonment of Eastern State Penitentiary and a revamping of the state's penal system at a cost of nearly twenty million dollars. The measure would establish a new Pennsylvania Correctional Diagnostic and Classification Center and locate a new maximum-security facility at Graterford.[61] But action on these matters was nearly a decade away, with blame for its glacial pace cast in various directions by the Department of Welfare, a grand jury, the warden and his staff, the prison trustees, and prominent politicians.

One suggestion made by Barnes and his associates seems prescient today. Eastern State Penitentiary was "one of the two great historic prisons of the world," they claimed. The State Prison at Auburn, New York, was by then demolished, except for its outside walls, but Cherry Hill was almost intact:

In penological history, the Eastern Penitentiary is as important as Independence Hall in our political history. But it is high time to recognize that its value and virtues are, today, exclusively historic.... Part of the present Eastern Penitentiary, especially a couple of the best preserved of the original wings or cell blocks, could well be retained as a national penological museum.[62]

Recognition of a different aspect of its historic value was voiced in 1946 by Fiske Kimball, director of the Philadelphia Museum of Art and a leading authority on the history of American architecture. "While most people don't think of the Pen in relation to beauty," he wrote in an editorial printed in the Philadelphia *Evening Bulletin*, "the exterior of this building is one of the most notable works of architecture in the United States.... It would be a great pity if those walls could not be preserved—even restored by the removal of the wretched barbican added to the entrance under WPA."[63]

Plans for change, meanwhile, circulated through Harrisburg and Phila-

Chart of crimes committed by the inmates incarcerated in Cherry Hill and Graterford as of 1927–28. From *Annual Report,* **1928.**

CRIMES

The 1753 prisoners now serving sentences in the Eastern State Penitentiary and the New Eastern State Penitentiary were convicted of the following crimes:—

	Sentenced Prior to June 1, 1927	June 1, 1927 to May 31, 1928 Received	Discharged	Remaining
Arson & Mal. Burning	19	13	9	23
Assault & Battery	0	47	19	28
Attempt to Dynamite	0	1	0	1
Bigamy	1	1	0	2
Breaking Jail	4	8	3	9
Breaking & Entering	0	19	7	12
Burglary	218	86	79	225
Conspiracy	6	3	1	8
Counterfeiting	0	1	0	1
Embezzlement	4	3	1	6
Extortion	0	3	1	2
False Pretense	4	0	3	1
Felonious Assault	84	10	18	76
Felonious Entry	128	62	76	114
Forgery	24	23	16	31
Fornication	0	1	0	1
Fraudulent Conversion	1	0	1	0
Horse Stealing	1	0	1	0
Issueing Worthless Checks	3	0	1	2
Incest	1	0	1	0
Kidnapping	1	0	0	1
Larceny	199	178	108	269
Malicious Mischief	0	1	0	1
Manslaughter	56	18	20	54
Mayhem	1	0	0	1
Murder	342	66	37	371
Obstructing R. R. Tracks	5	1	0	6
Pandering	5	4	3	6
Perjury	0	2	0	2
Pointing Revolver	1	0	1	0
Rape	132	38	30	140
Poss. of Burglar Tools	0	1	0	1
Rec. Stolen Goods	14	12	11	15
Robbery	277	116	80	313
Selling Drugs	2	0	0	2
Sodomy and Buggery	30	8	9	29
Total	1563	726	536	1753

Accommodation and Redefinition in the Twentieth Century

View to the north, over the east wall of the penitentiary, showing Corinthian Avenue and Girard College. Photograph, 1993, by Mark Perrott.

Aerial view of Eastern State Penitentiary from the south-southeast. Photograph, 1954, by the 111th Fighter Bomber Wing, Pennsylvania National Guard.

VI CRUCIBLE OF GOOD INTENTIONS

Interior of the upper level of cellblock five, showing a food cart on rails and the cast-iron Aeolic capitals of the original balustrade. Photograph, 1994, by Graydon Wood.

delphia. Demolition was assumed: 40 percent of those polled in 1946 by the *Evening Bulletin* desired some sort of recreation center at the site; 25 percent preferred a housing development. A year later, a new governor scrapped his predecessor's program and proposed a similar one (with different allocations) for a classification center to be built near Harrisburg and a new maximum-security facility added to Graterford.[64] Finally, in August 1953, the state legislature passed a law transferring prison administration from the Department of Welfare to a new Bureau of Correction in the Department of Justice. The new Commissioner of Corrections, Arthur T. Prasse, was given the authority to set apart portions of the two state penitentiaries for correctional, diagnostic, and classification purposes, and the long-planned reconfiguration of Eastern State Penitentiary finally went into effect at the start of the following year. A pamphlet issued then connected this new effort to "the humanity and hopefulness" of the old Pennsylvania system.[65]

Eastern State Penitentiary was to be the site of two entities: the State Correctional Institution at Philadelphia, or SCIPHA, a new maximum-security prison for 500 inmates; and the Eastern Correctional Diagnostic and Classification Center, or ECDCC, one of two centers statewide devised for study, classification, and assignment of new prisoners. The ECDCC operated cellblock fourteen and its nearby yard as a place of relative segrega-

tion from the rest of the prison population. Fraternization was restricted, although meals and the use of the clinic, chapel, and visiting facilities were shared with SCIPHA. New arrivals spent about eight weeks there. During its first six months of operation in 1954, the ECDCC received 678 convicts, with more than two-thirds then transferred to other institutions. Staff offices for the diagnostic center were installed in block three (the former hospital block) and in the administration building.[66] Over the next decade the combined facility would continue to accommodate about 1,000 inmates, roughly three-quarters of them in SCIPHA and the remainder in ECDCC.

New emphasis was placed on diagnostic and rehabilitative programs, and the resources devoted to them increased dramatically, but the administrative redefinition did not result in major changes to the physical plant, or in new use of space: block fourteen had been devoted to receiving and classification since 1934. The renovation begun a few years earlier was continued, providing upgraded service systems, rebuilt shower rooms, and new metal staircases. The most visible result of this campaign was the removal in 1951 of the old, wood-shingled central observation tower, which was dismantled and replaced with one of corrugated metal sheathing on a steel frame.[67] The image of modernity casting off stolid vestiges even extended to the new clock face, with brightly contrasting arabic numbers in place of the dimmer roman numerals.

Other improvements were planned. A new range of 34 punishment cells, block fifteen, was begun in 1956. After it opened in 1959, the older 10-cell punishment range known as block thirteen (attached to block ten) was no longer used. A new chapel-auditorium to replace the one improvised in the industrial building was projected as early as 1953, at an estimated cost of $220,000; the state finally made an appropriation for it in late 1959, and preliminary plans drawn by Albert F. Dagit the following year show a long rectangular building replacing the eastern portion of cellblock two. Working drawings and specifications were produced, but the project never materialized. In 1964 an improved visiting room was built to designs by architects Keast & Hemphill. This was located in the basement of the east side of the administration building, and extended as a one-story structure filling the original site of the warden's walled garden.[68]

A new warden, William A. Banmiller, took office in October 1956. He presented a sharp contrast to his predecessor, Walter Tees, who was remembered mainly for his toughness, his control of the "goon squad," and as "not at all treatment oriented."[69] The new warden emphasized rehabilitation and education: "A man was sent here as punishment," Banmiller stated, "not for punishment."[70] He recognized that 95 percent of his charges would be returned to society; he viewed his job as getting them ready. He worked in effective partnership with one of his subordinates, Joseph R. Brierly. Brierly was a direct, practical prison man hired by "Hardboiled" Smith in 1940. He prided himself on his toughness and honesty but had been drawn to classroom study of modern penology and psychology by Professors Teeters and Shearer and was sympathetic to new approaches. He greatly facilitated Banmiller's goals by maintaining the firm discipline that underpinned the new programs and freedoms. During Banmiller's tenure, movies were shown three times a week, there was evening "yard out" in summer, and two hours of television were permitted each night. Other innovations included an outdoor art course and night-school classes.[71]

When a major riot of about three dozen inmates broke out early in 1961, it was Brierly who took decisive and effective control, putting into effect his emergency plan, "Operation Breakout," which immediately brought in the state police. Then he quickly restored the normal routine, including group meals, for the vast majority of inmates who had not been involved, eliciting derision from some officials but quiet cooperation from the inmates.[72] The riot spurred renewed criticism of the antiquated structure and its residential location, bringing forth another flurry of proposals for its replacement. A task force appointed by the legislature began a three-year study. Claiming that Pennsylvania's "contribution to the science of corrective penology in modern times has been negligible,"[73] the study recommended more psychiatric and psychological services, along with sweeping reforms of the county prison system. In 1965 the legislature acted on the proposals, detailing measures for replacing Cherry Hill with a new, five-part complex at another site, combining a facility for reception and guidance, a medical center, a correctional treatment center, a personnel-training institute, and a correctional research facility. The old buildings were to be sold to the city for recreational or other use.[74]

Once more, however, action lagged far behind intention. The plan to relocate to a large site near Downingtown was defeated in 1967 by Republican legislators from that area. The City of Philadelphia was offered the Cherry Hill facility if it would help find a replacement site, and parcels near Fort Mifflin on the Delaware River and in southwest Philadelphia were considered as recently as 1970.[75]

In the interim, important changes were made at Eastern State Penitentiary. The institution was desegregated, with relatively little difficulty or public notice, in the 1960s. Brierly became warden (now known as the superintendent) in 1966. And a redesigned program for the institution was announced in 1968, in fulfillment of the 1965 legislative act. The program, devised by Brierly and Joseph F. Mazurkiewicz, the new director of treatment services, overturned the 1954 notion of the ECDCC and SCIPHA as separate institutions; the whole was to become a correctional treatment center. Inmates found to be intractable, including the "hard core" and those on death row, would be transferred out. There would be a change in climate from a maximum-security custodial function to one of intensive diagnosis and treatment, the nucleus of the new institution. The program would already be in place when a new facility elsewhere or improved facilities at the present site should become available. Formal therapy, casework, and pre-release programs were projected. More intensive efforts would be devoted to counseling, education, and training. The involvement of local academics in these activities and in research was encouraged. In the eleventh hour for the institution, a last effort was made to revive the more positive aspects of its founding spirit.[76]

But in September 1969 it was announced that the prison would close in one year. Nearly half of the 800 inmates were to be sent to the facility at Graterford, where there were vacant cells, and the others to appropriate institutions when their classification was completed. The staff of 235 was offered the chance to transfer. Better recreational and training opportunities at Graterford, excessive maintenance costs at Cherry Hill, and a shortage of staff in the correctional system were cited as reasons for the decision, but Warden Brierly singled out the opposition of Commissioner of Corrections Arthur T. Prasse to Eastern's new programs.[77] The penitentiary closed officially in January 1970, leaving behind only a maintenance force of 43 prisoners; by April the last of them were gone.

Aftermath

These were not the last prisoners at Eastern State Penitentiary. The state agreed to lease the facility to the city for one dollar, removing the stipulation that they provide a new site but adding conditions about renovating the structure and paying off state bonds for recent improvements. Almost immediately, the city needed the cells. A violent riot in early July 1970 at the city's critically overcrowded prison at Holmesburg (itself designed in the 1890s after the model of Eastern State Penitentiary) led to the transfer of prisoners to Cherry Hill. In 1971 there were hundreds, some convicted and others detained while awaiting trial. The state declined, however, to finalize the planned sale to the city until the city agreed to make a comprehensive study of correctional needs. The lease continued until the sale was finally concluded several years later.[78]

After the sale, debate over the use of the site resumed with greater fervor. The City Planning Commission involved itself, and the city transferred the property to the Redevelopment Authority in 1984.[79] Leading proposals for the site included a new justice center, redevelopment for housing, a recreation facility, and a supermarket. But precipitous action was forestalled by a lack of strong consensus for these proposals, by more active involvement of the neighboring community, by the reluctance of developers to take on the difficulties of adapting or demolishing the prison, and, most importantly, by a new appreciation of the prison's historical importance. Cherry Hill was certified as an historic site by the city in 1958 and placed on the state Register of Historic Places in 1970. It was accorded the more rarified status of a National Historic Landmark in 1965.[80] From the 1950s through the 1980s a host of publications brought the penitentiary to the attention of wider scholarly audiences in the fields of sociology, architecture, and American history, firmly placing it in the canon of the nation's most important sites.[81] The search for a viable and articulate future for the penitentiary has since dominated discussions of its fate.

Cell interior in cellblock one. Photograph, 1994, by Graydon Wood.

Attributed to William Langenheim (1807–1874) and Frederick Langenheim (1809–1879), *Front Entrance of Eastern State Penitentiary*, c. 1855. Salted-paper print, diameter 6¾". George Eastman House, Rochester, New York.

VII
The Legacy of Cherry Hill

NORMAN JOHNSTON

Attributed to William and Frederick Langenheim, *Rear of the Administration Building at Eastern State Penitentiary*, c. 1855. Salted-paper print, diameter 6¾". George Eastman House, Rochester, New York.

The well-intentioned attempt made at Eastern State Penitentiary to reform criminals and deter crime lasted for 142 years. How are we to judge this long-lived experiment in rehabilitation launched by Philadelphia prison reformers in the 1820s? To arrive at an answer, it is necessary to gauge the founders' social context and our own: first, through a comparison of Cherry Hill with other contemporary and modern prisons; and second, in terms of the prison's impact on the subsequent history of penal institutions in the United States and abroad.

The Rediscovery of Solitary Confinement

The system of solitary confinement used at Cherry Hill was controversial from its inception. Popular opinion today generally regards it as a cruel form of punishment, unlikely to have reformed or even deterred the criminal—a discredited relic of an earlier time. It is tempting to be shocked by its severity and smug in the assumption that we have progressed beyond such inhumane practices. However, cellular isolation never disappeared from prison regimens. It continued to be used in all prison systems as institutional punishment for rule infractions. Increasingly in the United States in the twentieth century, as prisoners became more violent and disruptive, solitary confinement was maintained as a form of quarantine, a way to remove inmates from the general prison population and to place them in more restrictive environments—prisons within prisons. This isolation was not intended to rehabilitate the inmate but rather to separate out the most dangerous prisoners and make the larger system easier to operate.

In 1934 the federal government opened Alcatraz Penitentiary on the island site of a Civil War fort, later a military prison, in San Francisco Bay. It was meant to house troublemakers and those prone to escape from other prisons in the federal system. There were no educational or vocational programs, family visits were limited, and there was no opportunity for parole. When Alcatraz became outmoded and too

VII Crucible of Good Intentions

costly to operate, it was replaced by a super-security federal prison in Marion, Illinois.

As Cherry Hill was closing its doors in the 1970s, separate "control units" or "special treatment units" for violent offenders were being added to existing high-security prisons, with very little disclosure to the public; in some cases, wholly new prisons were planned for this purpose. In such facilities, the movement of prisoners was restricted and inmates were handled individually or in very small groups. These prisons have come to be known as "maxi-maxi" or "super max" units and have all the trappings of new technology and nomenclature, although the methods used are hardly novel.[1]

Perhaps the best known of these new prisons is the Security Housing Unit (SHU) of the Pelican Bay State Prison in a remote region of northern California. Gang members and those who have committed violence against officers or other inmates while incarcerated may be sent to the Pelican Bay SHU. The regimen and architecture at Pelican Bay are typical of such super-security prisons.

Inmates are housed individually in bare concrete cells seven and a half feet wide by eleven and a half feet long, with concrete bunks. In each cell, a table and chair, also of concrete, are molded into the wall and floor, within inches of the toilet. There are no windows. Prisoners have no jobs, no educational program, and no group religious worship. They are not allowed to have watches, and other personal possessions are restricted: toothpaste is measured into a paper cup, toothbrush handles are clipped to a one-inch length, and candy bars have their wrappers removed. Meals are served in the cells after the food trays have been x-rayed. Inmates exercise individually in a yard ten feet wide and twenty-six feet long, which is covered by a metal grille and a plastic shield. Before they are led to the exercise yard, they are stripped, their clothing is searched, and their hands are cuffed behind their backs. Three times a week prisoners undergo the same procedure when they are taken one at a time for showers. If several prisoners are marched to a location such as the law library, they are chained together. Cell occupants are counted hourly around the clock.

When an inmate refuses a transfer to another cell or fails to return his food tray or salt and pepper, a "cell extraction" may be ordered, when four or five guards in riot gear immobilize the prisoner with Mace, stun guns,[2] or devices that fire rubber or wooden bullets. The inmate may then be placed in one of the "violence control cells," sometimes naked and hogtied in the fetal position for hours. These cells are lighted twenty-four hours a day, and the prisoner may remain in that section for one to three months.[3]

As at Cherry Hill in the 1830s, a primary accusation against some maxi-maxi prisons, and particularly Pelican Bay, is the allegation of psychological harm done to its inmates, either by exacerbating existing mental states or by fostering illness where none existed before. It is claimed that at least one-third of the occupants of the Pelican Bay SHU are psychotic during some part of their confinement there.[4] The psychological symptoms noted at Pelican Bay have been observed in similar units in federal and other state prisons.

The establishment of these new super-maximum-security facilities shows that the impulse to isolate prisoners and carefully control their behavior did not end with the demise of the Pennsylvania system. In these facilities we encounter single-cell occupancy, solitary exercise yards, eating in the cell, lack of group religious services, significant restrictions on contacts with the outside world, and accusations of prison-induced mental disturbances. Although these characteristics superficially resemble those of the old Pennsylvania system of separate confinement, there are fundamental differences. Most importantly, the SHUs and maxi-maxi prisons are devoid of the idealism and high hopes of the Quaker-inspired experiment in Philadelphia. If their means are not dissimilar, the purposes and principles to which they are applied could not be more different. These new isolation prisons are designed to hold the "worst of the worst" in the penal system, the sole expectation being that during the period of isolation, the inmates will injure no guards or other inmates and cause no disruptions or difficulties for prison administrators. Reform, vocational training, and preserving the sanity of the prisoners are not goals of these new prisons. The level of stark efficiency and cruelty characterizing these high-tech prisons are not in any way comparable to the unintended harshness of Cherry Hill's solitary regimen.

The Penitentiary as a Success

This most recent incarnation of the use of solitary confinement does, however, provide a lens through which we can view more clearly the scope of what was attempted at Cherry Hill, its context, its intentions, and its accomplishments. Max Grünhut, the distinguished European criminologist, has characterized penal history as "a history of ideals and errors."[5] Cherry Hill had an abundance of both, but the mistakes and inadequacies should not obscure its substantial successes, especially when compared with its immediate predecessor in Philadelphia, the Walnut Street Jail, and other eighteenth- and early-nineteenth-century prisons in North America and Europe. Those institutions had wrestled with problems that seem remarkably unchanged even today: many prisoners were tough and disruptive, much scheming went on with the jailers and behind their backs, overcrowding was chronic, and prisoners, mingling with one another, seemed to become more criminal rather than less during their incarceration. To address these problems Philadelphia's prison reformers conceived the first large-scale use of separate confinement and sought an architecture equal to their ambitions.

Main facade of Eastern State Penitentiary, late 1920s, showing the original front gate.

Prisons have proved to be troublesome projects for most architects, who are doubtless less familiar with the details of prison life than they are with those of more accessible buildings such as schools, hospitals, and offices. Haviland was a relatively inexperienced architect when he was commissioned to design the penitentiary in Philadelphia. At this early stage of his career, he was bold to assume so complex a project in a genre in which other capable and creative architects, much more experienced, had faltered. Robert Mills, Benjamin Henry Latrobe, William Strickland, and Charles Bulfinch in America, and George Dance the Younger in Britain, had all designed structures that—although their facades might have been greatly admired—proved to be unsatisfactory as prisons.[6]

Haviland had to design a prison that would forestall the disorders and abuses of the past and allow true cellular isolation around the clock. As an émigré British architect, he had available to him many examples of radial plans used for jails and asylums in his own and other European countries. The radial model was still, however, untested on such an ambitious project. Few of these institutions had been designed for complete solitary confinement, night and day; their purpose was to provide improved surveillance and control over their occupants. Accounts of the time, moreover, suggest that they were not particularly effective even in this respect.

The plan Haviland proposed for Eastern State Penitentiary was similar to those early radial structures, with short wings attached to a central unit, containing service facilities. As construction began at Cherry Hill, the initial plan was modified so that the center became a point of control and observation over the activity of the staff. Later, when the rigid system of isolation relaxed, the movements of inmates throughout the prison could be observed. With these adaptations, Haviland's design realized—perhaps for the first time—the full potential of the radial plan. For its combined improvements in efficiency of movement, security, surveillance, and ease of expansion, the design seemed to provide an unparalleled instrument for the implementation of the reformers' goals.

Not only did Haviland develop a general plan well-suited to the system of confinement at Cherry Hill, but he also devoted a great deal of care to details of the cells, an area often neglected by other prison architects. Cherry Hill cells were large compared to other prisons, and Haviland's innovative measures to contend with heating, ventilation, and waste disposal within the limitations of early-nineteenth-century technologies were distinct improvements over the systems in many buildings of the time. Throughout the entire prison the architect insisted on a high standard of construction, including fireproof vaulting for the cells and corridors—particularly significant for a building where people were locked in.

Prominently located on the periphery of a city that soon would surround it, Cherry Hill was meant to be seen. More than that, it was meant to communicate its purpose and its warning to the thousands who passed by or attended its tours. Haviland therefore dressed his design in an austere gothic style linked in the public mind to castles and cathedrals, historic symbols of power and authority as well as the sites of courts and prisons in Europe in earlier times. The choice of this evocative style (so maligned for its expense) to clothe an institution within which the coercive power of the state was striving to change criminal behavior was entirely appropriate, even inspired, for the noble experiment initiated within its walls.

Did Eastern State Penitentiary live up to the expectations of its founders? The answer, at least for the nineteenth century, must be a qualified "yes." The prison did indeed remedy most of the unsavory conditions of earlier institutions: insurrections, inmate victimization, general disorder, and frequent escapes were largely eliminated, as was the formation of a prisoner subculture with all of its contaminating influences. Cherry Hill had come to grips, albeit imperfectly, with one of the central problems of incarceration in all periods: the likelihood that inmates would be worsened by their daily contacts with other prisoners.

The question of how effectively the prison reformed its inmates is not so easily answered for a period when reliable information about the subsequent careers of released prisoners is simply not available. Assessments of successes and failures to reform inmates were usually based on anecdotes or were borne out by the return of a former prisoner to the same prison. For this reason, comparisons between success rates of Cherry Hill and those of other prisons were equally flawed. Although one could reasonably assume that Cherry Hill was more effective at reforming criminal behavior than its predecessors, it is impossible, in the absence of central fingerprint files and national recordkeeping for the nineteenth century, to compare recidivism rates between prisons then or to measure them against those of the twentieth century.

In retrospect, the Pennsylvania system as it was practiced at Cherry Hill contained the seeds of its eventual dissolution. The high initial cost of construction, the inability of inmates doing handwork in separate cells to make products that could bring significant income to the institution, and the cost of maintaining the prison with outside workers rather than with free or cheap inmate labor doomed the system more effectively than the positing of abstract arguments about mental health or psychological cruelty. The lapses in the policy of separation were an outcome of the prison's limited funds and staff. In the face of inadequate resources, rising prison populations, criticism from proponents of competing systems, and political interference, Cherry Hill was never given a full chance to prove its effectiveness. In addition, as in all prisons before and since, inmates found ways to beat the system; had the founders and the architect chosen to design a prison without consideration for the well-being of its occupants, they easily could have curtailed corrupting associations between prisoners even further.

The Penitentiary as Prototype
For a few years after the completion of Cherry Hill, a number of states attempted a regimen of segregation in cells patterned after the Pennsylvania system. The State Prison at Auburn, New York, after a brief, disastrous experiment with solitary confinement in small cells, developed its own regimen of congregate work by day and confinement in individual cells by night. Maryland, Massachusetts, Maine, New Jersey, Virginia, and Rhode Island also tried the system of separate confinement, but the financial burden, the problems with physical and mental illness, and the limited income from inmates working in cells resulted in each state's subsequent adoption of the Auburn system. By 1858 only Cherry Hill was still adhering to the separate system. For this reason, the radial plan of Haviland's Philadelphia and Trenton prisons had limited influence in the United States. Some prisons were built on the radial design in the nineteenth century in the United States, and even fewer in the twentieth century, but in each of these, the cellblocks were not intended for complete solitary confinement.

Eastern State Penitentiary has been described by the prominent architectural historian Henry-Russell Hitchcock as America's first building to have a real influence abroad.[7] Indeed, on the strength of its worldwide influence on prisons in the nineteenth century, Cherry Hill's importance cannot be overestimated. Cherry Hill became the prototype for the majority of prisons built outside the United States until the mid-twentieth century. Both its architecture and the method of penal treatment developed there emerged as the preferred solutions to the problems faced by prison systems in Europe and throughout the world. In some cases, prisons abroad maintained regimens of cellular isolation and solitary exercise and worship into the 1950s.[8] The radial plan for prisons spread rapidly to Europe, Latin America, and Asia; in Belgium, Great Britain, Spain, China, and Japan nearly every prison built until the middle of the twentieth century was on a plan showing Haviland's influence.

As Cherry Hill, then the largest public building in the United States, began to attract international emissaries, travelers, and philanthropists, the citizens of Philadelphia and Pennsylvania could view with increased pride the penitentiary and the system they had created. Cherry Hill symbolized the energy, the reasoned efforts, and the optimism with which early-nineteenth-century America, and more specifically Philadelphia, attempted to contend with many of the consequences of the growing urban population and the beginnings of industrialization. The problems of dependency, mental illness, and criminality were increasingly being addressed by the creation of large residential institutions, of which the penitentiary was the most ambitious and the most famous. Few doubted that these new institutions would adequately solve the social ills of the period.[9] Good intentions, enormous resources, strong talent, and innovative architecture characterized most of the efforts at Cherry Hill, but the reform of its occupants remained as elusive a goal then as it does in today's prisons.

The Legacy of Cherry Hill

Eastern Penitentiary, Philadelphia, 1830s. Engraving with watercolor, 2¹⁵⁄₁₆ x 4¹³⁄₁₆". The Library Company of Philadelphia.

Why is Cherry Hill, its usefulness as a functioning prison long since eroded, of significance today? Several prisons of the past have enjoyed greater notoriety or association with historic events: the Bastille, Newgate, Alcatraz, and Devil's Island come to mind. But less infamous prisons have been far more significant in influencing the methods of treating criminals and the architecture of penal institutions. Among these, Eastern State Penitentiary, virtually the only early prison structure of national and international importance that has not been torn down, established the methods for penology that were, next to democratic government, Philadelphia's most important export. The impact of Cherry Hill's architecture was even more widespread.

Over three hundred prisons worldwide show the direct or indirect imprint of Haviland's Philadelphia and Trenton prisons. It is on the basis of both contributions that Cherry Hill must be considered the most influential prison ever built and arguably the American building most widely imitated in Europe and Asia in the nineteenth century. No other building form in the country until the modern skyscraper played such a seminal role.

Notes to the Text

Chapter I (pages 9–19)

1. Isaac Weld, Jr., *Travels through the States of North America, and the Provinces of Upper and Lower Canada, during the Years 1795, 1796, and 1797* (London: John Stockdale, 1799), p. 5.

2. Weld, *Travels*, 1799, pp. 7, 9.

3. [Duc François-Alexandre-Frédéric de la Rochefoucauld-Liancourt], *On the Prisons of Philadelphia, by an European* (Philadelphia: Moreau de Saint-Mery, 1796), pp. 6–7. French editions were published simultaneously: *Des Prisons de Philadelphie, par un Européen* (Paris: Du Pont; Philadelphia: Moreau de Saint-Mery, 1796).

4. George E. Thomas, Michael J. Lewis, and Jeffrey A. Cohen, *Frank Furness: The Complete Works* (New York: Princeton Architectural Press, 1991), pp. 58, 70, 71.

5. Penn described the colony as a "holy experiment" in a letter to James Harrison, dated August 25, 1681; he referred to Philadelphia as a "greene Country Towne" in instructions to his commissioners William Crispin, John Bezar, and Nathaniel Allen, on September 30, 1681. Both documents are in Richard S. Dunn and Mary Maples Dunn, eds., *The Papers of William Penn*, vol. 2, *1680–1684* (Philadelphia: University of Pennsylvania Press, 1982), pp. 108, 121.

6. B[enjamin] Henry Latrobe, *Anniversary Oration, Pronounced before the Society of Artists of the United States, by Appointment of the Society, on the Eighth of May, 1811* (Philadelphia: Bradford and Inskeep, 1811), p. 17.

7. Latrobe, *Anniversary Oration*, 1811, p. 27.

8. Russell F. Weigley, ed., *Philadelphia: A Three-Hundred-Year History* (New York: W. W. Norton, 1982), pp. 218, 280, 309.

9. Benjamin Davies, *Some Account of the City of Philadelphia, the Capital of Pennsylvania, and Seat of the Federal Congress; Of Its Civil and Religious Institutions, Population, Trade, and Government…* (Philadelphia: Richard Folwell, 1794), p. 10.

10. Davies, *Some Account*, 1794, p. 8.

11. George B. Tatum, *Penn's Great Town: Two Hundred and Fifty Years of Philadelphia Architecture Illustrated in Prints and Drawings* (Philadelphia: University of Pennsylvania Press, 1961), pp. 164–65.

12. "Some Account of the Markets of Philadelphia," *The Portfolio*, vol. 2, no. 6 (December 1809), pp. 508–11.

13. Kenneth Finkel, "Public Architecture and the Emergence of Public Avenues in Philadelphia, 1800–1920," M.A. thesis, Temple University, 1978. See also [Samuel Hazard], *Facts in Relation to the Progressive Increase, Present Condition, and Future Prospects, of Philadelphia, as Connected with the Permanent Location of Public Buildings* (Philadelphia: J. Sharp, 1838).

14. Tatum, *Penn's Great Town*, 1961, p. 167. In transportation as well, obsolescence came rapidly. Pennsylvania had two hundred turnpike companies with three thousand miles of roads, but these were obsolete by the mid-1820s. The newly formed Pennsylvania Society for the Promotion of Internal Improvements had assumed canals to be the new cutting edge of transportation and hired architect William Strickland to study the matter. In his *Reports on Canals, Railways, Roads, and Other Subjects* (Philadelphia: H. C. Carey and I. Lea, 1826), Strickland concluded that railroads, not canals, were the coming trend in transportation.

15. *United States Gazette*, November 6, 1829. Quoted in Weigley, *Philadelphia*, 1982, p. 275.

16. Weigley, *Philadelphia*, 1982, pp. 270–71. The ship had one hundred and twenty guns.

17. Edwin Wolf II, "The Origins of Philadelphia's Self-Depreciation, 1820–1920," *The Pennsylvania Magazine of History and Biography*, vol. 104, no. 1 (January 1980), pp. 58–73.

18. Charles Dickens, *American Notes for General Circulation* (London: Chapman and Hall, 1842), vol. 1, pp. 234, 235.

19. Robert Montgomery Bird, *The City Looking Glass: A Philadelphia Comedy, in Five Acts* (New York: Colophon, 1933), p. 48. The play, written in July 1828, was not published until this edition of 1933 and was first performed publicly in January 1933. The cited passage, nevertheless, conveys the impact of the penitentiary's construction on the popular culture of Philadelphia in the late 1820s.

20. John M. Duncan, *Travels through Part of the United States and Canada in 1818 and 1819* (Glasgow: University Press, 1823), p. 194.

21. Cephas G[rier] Childs, *Views in Philadelphia and Its Environs, from Original Drawings Taken in 1827–30* (Philadelphia: C. G. Childs, 1827–30), unpaginated. William Strickland and John Haviland either designed or worked on ten of the twenty-two buildings depicted in Childs's series. For additional views, see Thomas Porter, *Picture of Philadelphia, from 1811 to 1831: Giving an Account of the Improvements of the City, during that Period: Embracing the Public Buildings, the House of Refuge, Prison, New Penitentiary, Widows', and Orphans' Asylum, Fair Mount Water Works, Etc.* (Philadelphia: Robert Desilver, 1831).

22. Childs, *Views in Philadelphia*, 1827–30, unpaginated.

23. Weigley, *Philadelphia*, 1982, pp. 289–90.

24. [Robert Waln, Jr.], *The Hermit in America on a Visit to Philadelphia: Containing Some Account of the Human Leeches, Belles, Beaux, Coquettes, Dandies, Cotillion Parties, Supper Parties, Tea Parties, Etc. Etc. of that Famous City; and the Poets and Painters of America*, 2nd ed. (Philadelphia: M. Thomas, 1819), p. 102.

25. For more on Clay's imagery, see Nancy Reynolds Davison, "E. W. Clay: American Political Caricaturist of the Jacksonian Era," Ph.D. diss., University of Michigan, 1980.

26. John F[anning] Watson, *Annals of Philadelphia, Being a Collection of Memoirs, Anecdotes, and Incidents of the City and Its Inhabitants from the Days of the Pilgrim Founders: Intended to Preserve the Recollections of Olden Time ... and the City in Its Local Changes and Improvements* (Philadelphia: E. L. Carey and A. Hart, 1830), p. 152.

27. Weigley, *Philadelphia*, 1982, p. 301. See also Constance M. Greiff, *Independence: The Creation of a National Park* (Philadelphia: University of Pennsylvania Press, 1987), pp. 35–36; and Charles B. Hosmer, Jr., *Presence of the Past: A History of the Preservation Movement in the United States before Williamsburg* (New York: G. P. Putnam's Sons, 1965), pp. 30–31.

28. *United States Gazette*, April 18, 1836, and October 17, 1839. Quoted in Weigley, *Philadelphia*, 1982, p. 284.

Chapter II (pages 21–29)

1. Tocqueville to Mme Edouard de Tocqueville, October 18, 1831. Quoted in George [Wilson] Pierson, *Tocqueville and Beaumont in America* (New York: Oxford University Press, 1938), p. 458. In full, the quote reads, "Philadelphia, beyond all others, is infatuated to the last degree with the penitentiary system, and as the penitentiary system is our *industry*, they vie with each other in pampering us."

2. Quoted in Frederick Howard Wines, *Punishment and Reformation: A Study of the Penitentiary System*, new ed., rev. and enl. (New York: Thomas Y. Crowell, 1919), p. 149. See also Thorsten Sellin, "Dom Jean Mabillon: A Prison Reformer of the Seventeenth Century," *Journal of the American Institute of Criminal Law and Criminology*, vol. 17, no. 4 (February 1927), p. 592.

3. Certainly one of the civil courts' earliest uses of imprisonment as punishment was in a Florentine prison known as Le Stinche, opened in 1304. See Marvin E. Wolfgang, "A Florentine Prison: Le Carceri delle Stinche," *Studies in the Renaissance*, vol. 7 (1960), pp. 148–66. For a description of Dutch workhouses, see Thorsten Sellin, *Pioneering in Penology: The Amsterdam Houses of Correction in the Sixteenth and Seventeenth Centuries* (Philadelphia: University of Pennsylvania Press, 1944). These establishments were also used occasionally as punishment for ungovernable sons of the well-to-do.

4. By the 1500s castles had largely lost their strategic value in military operations, but had not yet assumed antiquarian or historic value. They thus offered substantial, readily available space that could be devoted to prison use with little modification.

5. See Joseph Adshead, *Prisons and Prisoners* (London: Longman, Brown, Green, and Longman, 1845), p. 153n.

6. John Howard, *The State of the Prisons in England and Wales, with Preliminary Observations, and an Account of Some Foreign Prisons* (Warrington, England: William Eyres, 1777), p. 159.

7. Although often self-righteous and undiplomatically candid, Howard was well treated in his European travels, gaining entrance to most of the jails he sought, with the exceptions of the Catholic Church's Inquisition prisons and the Bastille. He posed as a doctor to enter Turkish prisons and chose to book passage on a ship that had not received medical clearance, knowing he would be detained in a plague hospital, so he could gain a first-hand picture of conditions there. Howard even smuggled scales into prisons to measure the bread rations of the prisoners. During his Russian travels in 1781 he was invited to court by Catherine the Great but opted instead for permission to visit prisons. See D. L. Howard, *John Howard: Prison Reformer* (New York: Archer House, 1958). Howard finally contracted gaol fever (typhus) while visiting military hospitals in the Crimea and died there in 1790.

8. John Howard, *An Account of the Principal Lazarettos in Europe; With Various Papers Relative to the Plague: Together with Further Observations on Some Foreign Prisons and Hospitals: And Additional Remarks on the Present State of Those in Great Britain and Ireland* (Warrington, England: William Eyres, 1789), p. 169n.

9. The miasmic theory of infection, popular at the time, suggested that filth could produce odors consisting of minute substances carried by the air and causing diseases in people who breathed this air. Proper ventilation, especially of buildings housing large numbers of people, consequently assumed great importance.

10. With Philadelphia's growth in population, jail commitments chronically outstripped existing capacity. The city's first jail, in the 1680s, was a cage—a strong, boxlike room, five feet by seven feet, at the corner of Second Street and what is now Market Street. Another prison, fourteen feet wide and twenty feet long, was erected between 1685 and 1695. Its inadequacy led to the building of the Old Stone Prison on the corner of Third and Market Streets in 1718. The cellar of the building now on that site contains what are probably vestiges of that original structure.

11. The criminologist Thorsten Sellin has concluded that the philosophy of using solitary confinement to prevent inmate contact had already been clearly stated before the Philadelphia reformers tried it at the Walnut Street Jail. See his "Origin of the 'Pennsylvania System of Prison Discipline,'" *The Prison Journal*, vol. 50, no. 1 (Spring/Summer 1970), pp. 19–20.

12. For a more detailed account of the development of the Pennsylvania-system philosophy see Negley K. Teeters and John D. Shearer, *The Prison at Philadelphia, Cherry Hill: The Separate System of Penal Discipline, 1829–1913* (New York: Columbia University Press, 1957), especially chap. 1. See also Teeters, *They Were in Prison: A History of the Pennsylvania Prison Society, 1787–1937 ...* (Philadelphia: John C. Winston, 1937); and Teeters, *The Cradle of the Penitentiary: The Walnut Street Jail at Philadelphia, 1773–1835* (Philadelphia: Pennsylvania Prison Society, 1955).

13. Teeters, *Cradle*, 1955, p. 31.

14. *The Pennsylvania Gazette*, September 26, 1787. Quoted in Teeters, *Cradle*, 1955, p. 132.

15. Teeters, *Cradle*, 1955. See also Harry Elmer Barnes, *The Evolution of Penology in Pennsylvania: A Study in American Social History* (Indianapolis: Bobbs-Merrill, 1927), especially chap. 3.

16. Howard had proposed raising jails on arches to control dampness and to deter prisoners from digging tunnels.

17. A contemporary description by Thomas Condie, from *The Philadelphia Monthly Magazine*, vol. 1 (February 1798), pp. 97–101, is cited in Teeters, *Cradle*, 1955, pp. 129–32. Teeters also reproduced a plan of the Walnut Street Jail, opposite p. 85.

18. [Duc François-Alexandre-Frédéric de la Rochefoucauld-Liancourt], *On the Prisons of Philadelphia, by an European* (Philadelphia: Moreau de Saint-Mery, 1796), p. 10. The simultaneous French editions *Des Prisons de Philadelphie, par un Européen* (Paris: Du Pont; Philadelphia: Moreau de Saint-Mery, 1796) gave international prominence to the Philadelphia experiment.

19. Thorsten Sellin, "Philadelphia Prisons of the Eighteenth Century," *Historic Philadelphia, from the Founding until the Early Nineteenth Century: Papers Dealing with Its People and Buildings, with an Illustrative Map*, special issue of *Transactions of the American Philosophical Society*, n.s., vol. 43, pt. 1 (March 1953), p. 329. Sellin examined the dockets for the years 1795 and 1796 and concluded that only a small number of the prisoners who qualified under the law to receive sentences served partly in solitary confinement in the Penitentiary House actually were given such sentences.

20. G[ustave] de Beaumont and A[lexis] de Tocqueville, *On the Penitentiary System in the United States, and Its Application in France; With an Appendix on Penal Colonies, and Also, Statistical Notes*, trans. Francis Lieber (Philadelphia: Carey, Lea and Blanchard, 1833), pp. 22, 51. Published as *Du Système pénitenciaire aux Etats-Unis, et de son application en France, suivi d'un*

appendice sur les colonies pénales, et de notes statistiques (Paris, 1833). The two young Frenchmen, aspiring members of the judiciary, thought it prudent to escape the complicated politics in their country and convinced their superiors to allow them to travel to America at their own expense to study various states' prison systems. Beaumont had a more abiding interest in prisons; Tocqueville developed a broader view and ultimately wrote *Democracy in America*.

21. *Letter, Report and Documents, on the Penal Code, from the President and Commissioners Appointed to Superintend the Erection of the Eastern Penitentiary, Adapted and Modelled to the System of Solitary Confinement* (Harrisburg, Pennsylvania: S. C. Stambaugh, 1828), p. 8.

22. *A Further Supplement to an Act, Entitled "An Act to Reform the Penal Laws of This Commonwealth"* (1829). Reprinted in [Thomas B. McElwee], *A Concise History of the Eastern Penitentiary of Pennsylvania, Together with a Detailed Statement of the Proceedings of the Committee, Appointed by the Legislature, December 6th, 1834* (Philadelphia: Neall and Massey, 1835), vol. 2, pp. 146–57.

23. *An Act to Provide for the Erection of a State Penitentiary within the City and County of Philadelphia* (1821). Reprinted in McElwee, *Concise History*, 1835, vol. 2, pp. 143–45.

Chapter III (pages 31–45)

1. *An Act to Provide for the Erection of a State Penitentiary within the City and County of Philadelphia* (1821). Reprinted in [Thomas B. McElwee], *A Concise History of the Eastern Penitentiary of Pennsylvania, Together with a Detailed Statement of the Proceedings of the Committee, Appointed by the Legislature, December 6th, 1834* (Philadelphia: Neall and Massey, 1835), vol. 2, pp. 143–45.

2. *Letter, Report and Documents, on the Penal Code, from the President and Commissioners Appointed to Superintend the Erection of the Eastern Penitentiary, Adapted and Modelled to the System of Solitary Confinement* (Harrisburg, Pennsylvania: S. C. Stambaugh, 1828), p. 13.

3. Prisons on a circular or semicircular plan for the most part were inspired by the proposal of the English philosopher Jeremy Bentham and his brother Sir Samuel Bentham, a naval architect, for the construction of circular prisons, factories, schools, and public institutions according to a design they named the Panopticon. This design, a rotunda with individual cells lined up along its periphery and facing inward, would provide both sanitary, humane conditions and total surveillance of the inhabitants from a vantage point at the rotunda's center. Although no true, full-circle panopticons were constructed in Great Britain, a number of small semicircular or polygonal structures were erected in England, Ireland, and Scotland after Jeremy Bentham's proposal was published in 1791, and especially in the 1820s.

Benjamin Henry Latrobe (with some input from Thomas Jefferson) was the first American architect to use the panopticon model, in his Virginia Penitentiary in Richmond, completed in 1800. This semicircular structure featured cells opening onto arcades on three levels. Strickland's plan for the Western Penitentiary two decades later may have been inspired by the prison of his former mentor Latrobe. Strickland's Western Penitentiary had cells back-to-back in a ring-shaped structure, an arrangement that, like Latrobe's design, did not permit surveillance of prisoners from a central point. Although Strickland's proposed plan for Eastern State Penitentiary has never been located, it was described as being similar to his Western Penitentiary.

True panopticons, with the central space and cells under one roof, were later built at three sites in Holland in 1884; at the Illinois State Penitentiary in Joliet, opened in 1919; and in Cuba on the Isle of Pines. See Norman Johnston, *The Human Cage: A Brief History of Prison Architecture* (New York: Walker, 1973), pp. 17–21.

4. The radial plan consisted of a center building, usually housing the head keeper, with several wings either connected to this hub or separated from it by ten to twenty feet, radiating like the spokes of a wheel. From the 1780s through the 1830s, some form of radial plan was virtually the only approved arrangement for the many county prisons built in Ireland and England, as well as some on the Continent. At the time Haviland submitted his proposal for Eastern State Penitentiary, radial plans had not been used for prisons in North America. For fuller discussion of the development of the radial plan see Norman Johnston, "John Haviland (1792–1852)," in Hermann Mannheim, ed., *Pioneers in Criminology*, 2nd ed., enl. (reprint, Montclair, New Jersey: Patterson Smith, 1972), pp. 107–28; and Johnston, "The Development of Radial Prisons: A Case Study in Cultural Diffusion," Ph.D. diss., University of Pennsylvania, 1958, especially pp. 150–78.

Some criminologists have suggested that Haviland's plan was probably inspired by two well-known penal institutions: the Maison de Force at Ghent, a Flemish workhouse completed in 1775; and Millbank Prison in London, built in 1813–21. Despite certain similarities of geometry, neither prison could have been the prototype for Haviland's radial plan. In both European prisons, a series of cellblocks, workshops, and administrative buildings were arranged around courtyards in contiguous polygons, to facilitate control over the inmates and to allow for the separation of various classes of prisoners. In form and use, their designs were closer to a series of connected, polygonal panopticons than to the single hub and straight ranges of cells of a true radial plan.

5. Minutes of meeting, May 14, 1822, "Book of Minutes of Board of Commissioners of the Eastern Penitentiary," pp. 139–41, Pennsylvania State Archives, Harrisburg. Quoted in Matthew Eli Baigell, "John Haviland," Ph.D. diss., University of Pennsylvania, 1965, p. 232.

6. See Negley K. Teeters and John D. Shearer, *The Prison at Philadelphia, Cherry Hill: The Separate System of Penal Discipline, 1829–1913* (New York: Columbia University Press, 1957), p. 43. Although published some time ago, this book remains the most important source of information about the prison and of documentation of the struggle among the Building Commissioners over Haviland and Strickland. Teeters and Shearer discovered, for example, that after one angry meeting of the commissioners, several pages were removed from the group's minutes book. The authors were able to reconstruct the events of the meeting from a draft they discovered in the archives of the prison.

7. See Teeters and Shearer, *Cherry Hill*, 1957, pp. 41–42.

8. Joseph Jackson, *Early Philadelphia Architects and Engineers* (Philadelphia: Privately printed, 1923), pp. 147–48. See also Sandra L. Tatman and Roger W. Moss, *Biographical Dictionary of Philadelphia Architects: 1700–1930* (Boston: G. K. Hall, 1985), p. 344. Morduinoff was an intimate of John Howard and was at Howard's bedside when he died of gaol fever (typhus) in the Crimea. Undoubtedly, Haviland heard much about the great reformer during his Russian visit. The Haviland Papers (Van Pelt Library, University of Pennsylvania, on loan from the Somerset Archaeological and Natural History Society, Taunton, England; hereafter cited as Haviland Papers) include a number of daybooks, spanning his career. Daybook 18 contains the description of Howard's funeral, eulogies, and an account of Morduinoff's friendship with the reformer.

9. In addition to the prisons already mentioned, Haviland designed the New Jersey State Prison, Trenton (1833–36); Allegheny County Courthouse and Jail, Pittsburgh (1834); Arkansas Penitentiary, Little Rock (1838); Dauphin County Prison, Harrisburg, Pennsylvania (1840–42); Berks County Prison, Reading, Pennsylvania (1846–48); and Lancaster County Prison, Lancaster, Pennsylvania (1849–51). He probably contributed to the plans for the two county prisons his son Edward built in York and Cumberland counties in Pennsylvania.

10. Haviland, October 11, 1842, daybook 6, Haviland Papers.

11. Haviland, "Explanation of a Design for a Penitentiary," July 2, 1821, daybook 1, p. [19], Haviland Papers.

12. For a brief description see Johnston, *Human Cage*, 1973, especially pp. 21–28. See also Robin Evans, *The Fabrication of Virtue: English Prison*

Architecture, 1750–1840 (Cambridge: Cambridge University Press, 1982).

13. The plan of the London Lunatic Asylum is reproduced in H[ermann] A[ugust] Adam, *Über Geisteskrankheit in alter und neuer Zeit: Ein Stück Kulturgeschichte in Wort und Bild* (Ansbach, Germany: C. Brügel und Sohn, [1928]), p. 29. The image is undoubtedly reproduced from an English engraving, but its source is given only as a collection of plans in private hands. A plan for the Cornwall Lunatic Asylum is reproduced in John Foulston, *The Public Buildings Erected in the West of England, As Designed by John Foulston . . .* (London: J. Williams, 1838), pl. 105, following p. 74.

14. The engraving by Cephas Grier Childs is the frontispiece to G[eorge] W[ashington] Smith, *A View and Description of the Eastern Penitentiary of Pennsylvania* (Philadelphia: C. G. Childs, 1830). This pamphlet also contains an engraving of the prison's facade.

15. Haviland, "Explanation of a Design for a Penitentiary," July 2, 1821, daybook 1, pp. [24–25], Haviland Papers.

16. Nikolaus Pevsner, *An Outline of European Architecture*, 5th ed. (Harmondsworth, England: Penguin Books, 1957), p. 269.

17. Both in literature and in architecture a gothic revival was sweeping Britain between 1790 and 1820. Sir Walter Scott's *Ivanhoe* appeared in 1819, and many publications reflected an interest in gothic cathedrals and antiquities. Early gothic-revival architecture was often inaccurate in detail and unfaithful in spirit. Haviland's work, though sometimes eclectic, was generally praised by the architectural community both at the time and in the twentieth century. He shunned elements of the picturesque and designed an austere, symmetrical exterior for Cherry Hill.

18. The most notable exceptions were his designs for the New Jersey State Prison at Trenton and the Tombs in New York City, both of which he clothed in an Egyptian-revival style. With these two designs Haviland is generally credited with introducing this style in the United States.

19. James Elmes, *Hints for the Improvement of Prisons, for Their Better Regulation, and for a More Œconomical Management of Prisoners; Partly Founded on the Principles of the Late John Howard, Esq. F.A.S.* (London: W. Bulmer, 1817), p. 14.

20. Minutes of meeting, March 26, 1822, "Book of Minutes of Board of Commissioners of the Eastern Penitentiary," p. 115, Pennsylvania State Archives, Harrisburg.

21. John Howard had written in 1789: "The new gaols, having pompous fronts, appear like palaces to the lower class of people in Ireland; and some persons object against them on this account, especially those who are obliged to contribute towards their expense, and think it would be better if they were less commodious." John Howard, *An Account of the Principal Lazarettos in Europe; With Various Papers Relative to the Plague: Together with Further Observations on Some Foreign Prisons and Hospitals: And Additional Remarks on the Present State of Those in Great Britain and Ireland* (Warrington, England: William Eyres, 1789), p. 78.

22. [William] Hepworth Dixon, *The London Prisons: With an Account of the More Distinguished Persons Who Have Been Confined in Them: To Which Is Added, A Description of the Chief Provincial Prisons* (London: Jackson and Walford, 1850), pp. 365–66.

23. [John Haviland], *A Description of Haviland's Design for the New Penitentiary Now Erecting near Philadelphia: Accompanied with a Bird's-eye View* (Philadelphia: Robert Desilver, 1824), p. 12. The position of the cornerstone is now unknown.

24. Teeters and Shearer (*Cherry Hill*, 1957, p. 63) stated that when the old gate was demolished, the oak planks were burned at the prison and the handwrought rivets were given to employees as souvenirs.

25. *A Further Supplement to an Act, Entitled "An Act to Reform the Penal Laws of This Commonwealth"* (1829). Reprinted in McElwee, *Concise History*, 1835, vol. 2, p. 146.

26. Accounts of the number of cells vary from one source to another. There seem to have been 450 cells upon the completion of block seven. However, Frédéric-Auguste Demetz and Guillaume-Abel Blouet indicated 464 occupied cells (*Rapports à M. le Comte de Montalivet, Pair de France, Ministre Secrétaire d'État au Département de l'Intérieur, sur les pénitenciers des Etats-Unis* [Paris: Imprimerie royale, 1837], p. 61), and other writers have suggested still larger numbers. Some of the cells were adapted for bathing; others were combined by removing partitions for use as a dispensary; and yet others were used for preparing food. Modifications were made frequently from the earliest days of the prison.

27. Early in the construction of the cellblocks Haviland had realized that his mechanical systems were inadequate. In a letter to the French commissioners Demetz and Blouet, he wrote: "But time and experience has taught me that there is still much to be learnt. Our Water Closet warming & ventilating apparatus were defective for although they answered admirably their direct purposes yet they proved instrumental in effecting an intercourse from cell to cell. . . ." Undated draft, probably written in the 1830s, daybook 1, pp. [172–73], Haviland Papers.

28. This system, developed and patented by Angier Perkins in England in 1831, was used in the British Museum, London, in 1835 and in the House and Senate wings of the U.S. Capitol in 1855. See Eugene S. Ferguson, "An Historical Sketch of Central Heating: 1800–1860," in Charles Peterson, ed., *Building Early America: Contributions toward the History of a Great Industry* (Radnor, Pennsylvania: Chilton, 1976), pp. 169–72. Haviland corresponded with Perkins but entered into no contractual agreement to use his patented system. The heating and ventilating of large buildings generally was unsatisfactory at the time, as descriptions of the problems in the U.S. Capitol and elsewhere make abundantly clear. Other large prisons, such as those in Sing Sing and Auburn, in New York State, had even less adequate heating and ventilating systems. For a description of Sing Sing prison, see [William Crawford], *Report of William Crawford, Esq., on the Penitentiaries of the United States, Addressed to His Majesty's Principal Secretary of State for the Home Department* [London: Parliamentary Papers, 1834], appendix p. 29.

29. Frederic Hill, *Crime: Its Amount, Causes, and Remedies* (London: John Murray, 1853), p. 261.

30. See Dr. Robert Given's observations in Teeters and Shearer, *Cherry Hill*, 1957, pp. 72–73.

31. Miercken had cashed a state draft for $20,000, inexplicably exchanging one $1,000 note for two $500 ones. The following day he carried the entire sum, in cash, in his trouser pocket to the Building Commissioners' meeting but discovered that he did not have it when he arrived. The next evening an envelope containing $15,000 supposedly was slipped into his warehouse. Several weeks later another packet with $4,000 was recovered with a note signed by a "Tom Find," indicating that the finder claimed $500 as a reward and that the remaining $500 was missing. The state auditor took no action. Six months later Miercken died insolvent. See Teeters and Shearer, *Cherry Hill*, 1957, pp. 37–40.

32. G[ustave] de Beaumont and A[lexis] de Tocqueville, *On the Penitentiary System in the United States, and Its Application in France; With an Appendix on Penal Colonies, and Also, Statistical Notes*, trans. Francis Lieber (Philadelphia: Carey, Lea and Blanchard, 1833), p. 74.

33. Teeters and Shearer (*Cherry Hill*, 1957, p. 74) cited figures from McElwee (*Concise History*, 1835, vol. 1, p. 199), who wrote his report before the prison was completed. Taking the overall cost—$772,000—and dividing it by the number of cells, Teeters and Shearer determined that each cell cost $2,500. However, the monies spent on the construction of the wall, front buildings, and rotunda were already included, and the completion of the remaining cellblocks (bringing the number of cells to 450) would have reduced the cost per cell to about $1,800. This is still very expensive compared with a prison built during the same time in Connecticut, at a cost of $151 per cell, or Sing Sing, at $200 per cell, both built with inmate labor. Professor Nicolaus Heinrich Julius determined that the cost per cell for Cherry Hill was $1,024, using a lower total cost than other published sources. N[icolaus] H[einrich] Julius, *Nordamerikas sittliche Zustände: Nach eigenen*

Anschauungen in den Jahren 1834, 1835, und 1836 (Leipzig: F. A. Brockhaus, 1839), vol. 2, p. 239.

34. Privately, Haviland may have become convinced that attached exercise yards were a poor idea because they reduced air circulation and sunlight and required the use of skylights instead of windows. Haviland deliberately eliminated attached yards in his design for the New Jersey State Prison at Trenton. Only in his last prison, erected in Lancaster County, Pennsylvania, between 1849 and 1851, did the architect again specify attached yards. Almost all of the European and Asian prisons influenced by Cherry Hill had detached exercise yards, situated well away from the cellblocks.

Chapter IV (pages 47–67)

1. Alexander Paterson, head of the British prison system in the 1940s. Quoted in Negley Teeters, "The Passing of Cherry Hill: Most Famous Prison in the World," *The Prison Journal*, vol. 50, no. 1 (Spring/Summer 1970), p. 8.

2. *A Further Supplement to an Act, Entitled "An Act to Reform the Penal Laws of This Commonwealth"* (1829). Reprinted in [Thomas B. McElwee], *A Concise History of the Eastern Penitentiary of Pennsylvania, Together with a Detailed Statement of the Proceedings of the Committee, Appointed by the Legislature, December 6th, 1834* (Philadelphia: Neall and Massey, 1835), vol. 2, p. 154. Early annual reports of the prison published single-paragraph descriptions of each entering prisoner, stating the causes of his behavior, his disposition, his receptivity to constructive ideas, his health, and the outlook for his future.

3. At first, hoods without eye holes were used for leading inmates through the prison. Later, as the prison began to employ inmates for maintenance tasks, hoods with eye holes were substituted, allowing the inmate worker to perform his duties but supposedly protecting his anonymity by shielding his face from other inmates.

Concern that a prisoner with knowledge of the layout of a prison poses a breach of security is still very much a part of the thinking of many prison officials. The U.S. Federal Bureau of Prisons, like many state prison bureaucracies, will not release plans of its prisons, revealing only block outlines without details, for "security reasons."

4. McElwee, *Concise History*, 1835, vol. 1, p. 215. This book represents, in essence, a minority report of the 1834–35 investigation. McElwee, the only dissenting member of the committee, had the book printed over the objections of the warden and at his own expense.

5. Harry Elmer Barnes and Negley K. Teeters, *New Horizons in Criminology: The American Crime Problem*, rev. ed. (New York: Prentice-Hall, 1945), p. 516.

6. See Negley K. Teeters and John D. Shearer, *The Prison at Philadelphia, Cherry Hill: The Separate System of Penal Discipline, 1829–1913* (New York: Columbia University Press, 1957), p. 78.

7. Frederick Wines, a nineteenth-century penologist, described the code as originating in Russian prisons and spreading to other countries. He suggested that the code was based on two groupings of raps as determined below:

	1	2	3	4	5
1	A	B	C	D	E
2	F	G	H	I	J
3	K	L	M	N	O
4	P	Q	R	S	T
5	U	V	W	X	Y
6	Z				

For example, three raps followed almost immediately by four would signify the letter *N*. Or sharp raps with knuckles and dull ones with the wrist would distinguish the vertical from the horizontal axis. Wines described solitary cells in a Russian fortress prison where cell floors and walls were covered with felt, and a wire netting covered with paper and cloth was strung five inches from the wall, all to prevent the use of knocking codes. Frederick Howard Wines, *Punishment and Reformation: A Study of the Penitentiary System*, new ed., rev. and enl. (New York: Thomas Y. Crowell, 1919), pp. 164–65.

8. *The Twenty-first Annual Report of the Inspectors of the Eastern State Penitentiary of Pennsylvania* (Philadelphia: Edmond Barrington and George D. Haswell, 1850), p. 26.

9. Charles Dickens, *American Notes for General Circulation* (London: Chapman and Hall, 1842), vol. 1, p. 246.

10. "Two Years in Prison," *The Philadelphia Press*, September 27, 1885.

11. McElwee, *Concise History*, 1835, vol. 1, p. 208.

12. [Michael John Cassidy], *Warden Cassidy on Prisons and Convicts: Remarks from Observation and Experience Gained during Thirty-seven Years' Continuous Service in the Administration of the Eastern State Penitentiary, Pennsylvania* (Philadelphia: Patterson and White, 1897), p. 61.

13. For the nineteenth-century working-class diet see Harvey A. Levenstein, *Revolution at the Table: The Transformation of the American Diet* (New York: Oxford University Press, 1988), chap. 2, especially p. 23.

14. McElwee, *Concise History*, 1835, vol. 1, pp. 164–65.

15. *First and Second Annual Reports of the Inspectors of the Eastern State Penitentiary of Pennsylvania, Made to the Legislature at the Sessions of 1829–30, and 1830–31* (Philadelphia: Thomas Kite, 1831), p. 9.

16. *First and Second Annual Reports* (1831), p. 11.

17. William Crawford observed American prisons during his visit beginning in 1833. [William Crawford], *Report of William Crawford, Esq., on the Penitentiaries of the United States, Addressed to His Majesty's Principal Secretary of State for the Home Department* [London: Parliamentary Papers, 1834], appendix p. 8.

18. Cassidy, *Warden Cassidy*, 1897, p. 79.

19. Teeters and Shearer (*Cherry Hill*, 1957, pp. 196–200) discussed some of the signers of the visitors' register, which is housed at the Pennsylvania State Archives, Harrisburg.

20. See William Roscoe, *A Brief Statement of the Causes Which Have Led to the Abandonment of the Celebrated System of Penitentiary Discipline, in Some of the United States of America: In a Letter to the Hon. Stephen Allen, of New-York* (Liverpool, England: Harris, 1827), p. 31. Roscoe quoted a letter to the editor published in a Washington, D.C., newspaper in which the writer recounted a conversation he had with Lafayette.

21. See Teeters and Shearer, *Cherry Hill*, 1957, p. 198.

22. The figures for 1835 and 1839 are cited in Teeters and Shearer (*Cherry Hill*, 1957, p. 196). The 1859 report of the prison inspectors stated that from 1854 through 1858, a total of 36,898 visitors signed the guest register but over 40,000 came to the prison, not including friends and relatives of the prisoners or people entering the prison on business. *Thirtieth Annual Report of the Inspectors of the State Penitentiary for the Eastern District of Pennsylvania* (Philadelphia: McLaughlin Brothers, 1859). The 1862–72 figure is from Richard Vaux, *Brief Sketch of the Origin and History of the State Penitentiary for the Eastern District of Pennsylvania, at Philadelphia* (Philadelphia: McLaughlin Brothers, 1872), p. 94.

23. Charles Dickens described Eastern State Penitentiary as "a most dreadful, fearful place" in a letter to his friend and agent, John Forster. Quoted in Philip Collins, *Dickens and Crime* (London: Macmillan, 1962), p. 120.

24. When Dickens was twelve, his father was jailed for debt in one of London's more infamous old prisons; later, prisons would figure prominently in many of his novels. Despite his family history and whatever view of the underclass and its criminals he might have suggested in his books, Dickens did not have much sympathy for adult offenders. He was a great friend of the governor of one of the London prisons that operated on the Auburn system, and in newspaper articles he attacked the separate system about to be established at the new Pentonville prison in London. See Collins, *Dickens and Crime*, 1962.

25. Quoted in Vaux, *Brief Sketch*, 1872, p. 111.

26. Quoted in John Forster, *The Life of Charles Dickens*, 4th ed. (London: Chapman and Hall, 1872), vol. 1, pp. 326, 327–28.

27. Dickens, *American Notes*, 1842, vol. 1, pp. 238–39.

28. Sidney P. Moss, *Charles Dickens' Quarrel with America* (Troy, New York: Whitston, 1984), p. 81.

29. Joseph Adshead, *Prisons and Prisoners* (London: Longman, Brown, Green, and Longman, 1845), p. 112.

30. Dickens, *American Notes*, 1842, vol. 1, p. 246.

31. William Peter, quoted in Negley Teeters, *They Were in Prison: A History of the Pennsylvania Prison Society, 1787–1937...* (Philadelphia: John C. Winston, 1937), p. 231.

32. *The Philadelphia Press*, March 21, 1884. Cited in Teeters and Shearer, *Cherry Hill*, 1957, pp. 118–22.

33. [William Tallack], *Charles Dickens' Prison Fictions* [London: Wertheimer, Lea, 1894?].

34. See Collins, *Dickens and Crime*, 1962, p. 132.

35. Harold Donaldson Eberlein, "When Society First Took a Bath," *The Pennsylvania Magazine of History and Biography*, vol. 67, no. 1 (January 1943), p. 47.

36. Pennsylvania Prison Society, "Acting Committee Minutes," vol. 3', April 10, 1846, p. 180, Library of the Pennsylvania Prison Society, Philadelphia.

37. *Forty-fifth Annual Report of the Inspectors of the State Penitentiary for the Eastern District of Pennsylvania... for the Years 1873 and 1874* (Philadelphia: Sherman, 1875), pp. 135, 136.

38. Case cited in Teeters and Shearer, *Cherry Hill*, 1957, p. 175.

39. *Forty-sixth Annual Report of the Inspectors of the State Penitentiary for the Eastern District of Pennsylvania... for the Year 1875* (Philadelphia: Sherman, 1876), p. 140.

40. *The Times* (London), November 25, 1843. Quoted in Adshead, *Prisons and Prisoners*, 1845, p. 19.

41. Crawford, *Report*, 1834, appendix p. 4.

42. A commission appointed by the New York Prison Association in 1846 reported that at Auburn prison, "we were struck by the great number of individuals affected by mental aberration, whose cases appeared to have quite escaped the doctor's observation." The commission added, "Cases of mental derangement are much more frequent in the prisons on the Auburn system than are mentioned in the reports." Quoted in Orlando F. Lewis, *The Development of American Prisons and Prison Customs, 1776–1845: With Special Reference to Early Institutions in the State of New York* (1922; reprint, Montclair, New Jersey: Patterson Smith, 1967), p. 249.

43. In Germany, where the Pennsylvania system was generally adopted, there was great concern about the incidence of psychotic disturbance among the prisoners, and numerous studies were published in nineteenth-century journals. For more see Stuart Grassian, "Psychopathological Effects of Solitary Confinement," *The American Journal of Psychiatry*, vol. 140, no. 11 (November 1983), pp. 1,450–51.

44. *Forty-sixth Annual Report* (1876), p. 146.

45. Perhaps McElwee's observations as a committee member for the 1834–35 investigation sum up the frustrations and reflect the difficulties of most prison investigations: "A convict in durance is not a credible witness. Do you look to the Inspectors and Wardens? The Inspectors may be deceived, and the Warden will not bear testimony against himself. Will you examine the under keepers? If they implicate the Warden or Inspectors, they are discharged.... How then can you arrive at the truth?" McElwee, *Concise History*, 1835, vol. 1, p. 21.

46. McElwee, *Concise History*, 1835, vol. 1, pp. 17, 167, 179.

47. McElwee, *Concise History*, 1835, vol. 1, pp. 17, 18.

48. McElwee, *Concise History*, 1835, vol. 1, pp. 18, 158, 159, 177–78.

49. Corporal punishment has continued to be used on occasion in U.S. prisons up to the present. The 1940 U.S. attorney general's survey of punishment practices in state prisons revealed that officials *admitted* to the Justice Department that they used whipping and the ball and chain for discipline. In 1980 the state of Louisiana was still using sweatboxes, small freestanding structures, sometimes of metal, with only enough room to stand and a hole in the floor as a toilet. Generally, in the late twentieth century, punishments such as beating with batons, gassing with tear gas, and handcuffing to cots have been used only after prison riots or disturbances, rather than for routine punishment for prison rule infractions. In 1989 when inmates were transferred to Graterford State Correctional Institution, in Pennsylvania, they were met by two lines of officers in riot gear. Later, prisoners testified in court that their legs were beaten with four-foot-long riot batons and that electric stun guns were used on some handcuffed inmates. The officers claimed they were under the mistaken impression that the inmates had participated in an earlier riot elsewhere.

50. McElwee, *Concise History*, 1835, vol. 1, p. 34.

51. Testimony printed in McElwee (*Concise History*, 1835, vol. 1) highlighted threats Mrs. Blundin made against the warden, saying that she would "flog that *damn quaker son of a bitch!*" (p. 211), knock every tooth down his throat, and break "every pane of glass in the Centre house" (p. 212).

52. Judge Coxe, February 1, 1834. Quoted in Teeters and Shearer, *Cherry Hill*, 1957, p. 107.

53. See Teeters and Shearer, *Cherry Hill*, 1957, pp. 107–10.

54. The routine developed by Warden Elam Lynds for the State Prison at Auburn, New York, and followed with minor variations through the nineteenth century, is described in G[ershom] Powers, *A Brief Account of the Construction, Management, and Discipline Etc. Etc. of the New-York State Prison at Auburn, Together with a Compendium of Criminal Law: Also a Report of the Trial of an Officer of Said Prison for Whipping a Convict* (Auburn, New York: U. F. Doubleday, 1826), especially pp. 5–10.

55. G[ustave] de Beaumont and A[lexis] de Tocqueville, *On the Penitentiary System in the United States, and Its Application in France; With an Appendix on Penal Colonies, and Also, Statistical Notes*, trans. Francis Lieber (Philadelphia: Carey, Lea and Blanchard, 1833), appendix p. 201.

56. Powers, *Brief Account*, 1826, p. 68.

57. See Eric C. Schneider, *In the Web of Class: Delinquents and Reformers in Boston, 1810s–1930s* (New York: New York University Press, 1992), pp. 102–3, 49.

58. Beaumont and Tocqueville, *On the Penitentiary System*, 1833, appendix p. 202.

59. *Sixty-seventh Annual Report of the Inspectors of the State Penitentiary for the Eastern District of Pennsylvania... for the Year 1896* (Philadelphia: Charles H. Elliott, 1897), p. 8.

Chapter V (pages 69–79)

1. In the nineteenth century, radial prisons were constructed in New Jersey (the New Jersey State Prison at Trenton, 1833–36, and the New Jersey Reformatory at Rahway, 1895–1908), Massachusetts (the Massachusetts Reformatory at West Concord, 1878), Michigan (the Michigan Reformatory at Ionia, 1878), Pennsylvania (the Pennsylvania Reformatory at Huntington, 1889, and the Philadelphia County Prison at Holmesburg, 1895–96), Kansas (the United States Penitentiary at Leavenworth, 1896–1928), and Ohio (the State Reformatory at Mansfield, 1896).

2. In the twentieth century, radial prisons were constructed in New Jersey (the New Jersey Youth Reception and Correction Center at Yardville, 1968), Oklahoma (the Oklahoma State Prison at McAlester, 1909), Hawaii (the Oahu Penitentiary, 1914), Indiana (the Indiana Reformatory at Pendleton, 1923), Pennsylvania (the Philadelphia House of Correction, 1926),

Kansas (the United States Disciplinary Barracks at Ft. Leavenworth, 1940), Washington (the Washington State Penitentiary at Walla Walla, 1954), Texas (the Coffield Unit at Tennessee Colony, 1979), Ohio (the Eastern Correctional Center at Maury, 1983, and the Southern Correctional Center at Troy, 1983), and at two locations in North Carolina.

3. [William Crawford], *Report of William Crawford, Esq., on the Penitentiaries of the United States, Addressed to His Majesty's Principal Secretary of State for the Home Department* [London: Parliamentary Papers, 1834], p. 3. See also Norman Johnston, introduction to *Report of William Crawford . . .* (1834; reprint, Montclair, New Jersey: Patterson Smith, 1969), pp. vii–xvii.

4. A massive prison rebuilding program, beginning with the construction of the Model Prison, followed the publication of Crawford's survey. An early chairman of commissioners of prisons stated that within six years of the model prison's completion at Pentonville fifty-four new prisons with a total of 11,000 cells were built. Edmund F. Du Cane, *The Punishment and Prevention of Crime* (London: Macmillan, 1885), p. 56.

5. Joseph Adshead, *Prisons and Prisoners* (London: Longman, Brown, Green, and Longman, 1845), pp. 256–57. In 1827 Julius had lectured in Berlin under the auspices of the newly formed Verein für die Besserung der Strafgefangenen, a prisoners' aid society. Then-Crown Prince Friedrich Wilhelm attended the lectures, and presumably became interested in prison reform at that time.

6. One observer in 1933 found roughly half of the inmates at the Zuchthaus in Straubing, Bavaria, working in solitary confinement in their cells. Inmates were confined in individual cubicles in the chapel during religious services. When American officials visited the prison in 1954, they noted that 10 percent of the prisoners at that time were working in their cells. See Norman S. Hayner, "German Correctional Procedures: Impact of the Occupation," *National Probation and Parole Association Journal*, vol. 1, no. 2 (October 1955), p. 172.

7. G[ustave] de Beaumont and A[lexis] de Tocqueville, *On the Penitentiary System in the United States, and Its Application in France; With an Appendix on Penal Colonies, and Also, Statistical Notes*, trans. Francis Lieber (Philadelphia: Carey, Lea and Blanchard, 1833). Published in France as *Du Système pénitenciaire aux Etats-Unis, et de son application en France, suivi d'un appendice sur les colonies pénales, et de notes statistiques* (Paris, 1833). See George [Wilson] Pierson, *Tocqueville and Beaumont in America* (New York: Oxford University Press, 1938).

8. Frédéric-Auguste Demetz and Guillaume-Abel Blouet, *Rapports à M. le Comte de Montalivet, Pair de France, Ministre Secrétaire d'Etat au Département de l'Intérieur, sur les pénitenciers des Etats-Unis* (Paris: Imprimerie royale, 1837).

9. La Santé prison, also in Paris, was erected between 1862 and 1867 on plans by Joseph-Auguste-Emile Vaudremer, who had trained under Emile Gilbert and G.-A. Blouet.

10. In 1866 in the state of Sardinia, for example, there was a total of 1,620 cells in four prisons run on the Auburn system and 1,160 cells in five prisons that had adopted the Pennsylvania system. Frederíco Bellazzi, *Prigioni e prigionieri nel regno d'Italia* (Florence: Tipografia Militare, 1866), p. 30.

11. [A. Salomon], *Notice sur l'histoire des prisons et de la réforme pénitentiaire en Russie* (St. Petersburg: L'administration générale des prisons, 1885), p. 14.

12. José Lemos Britto, *Os systemas penitenciarios do Brasil* (Rio de Janeiro: Imprensa nacional, 1925), vol. 2, pp. 176–81.

13. I am indebted to the Japanese Ministry of Justice and especially architect Fujitaro Kusunoki, formerly of the Bureau of Correction, for this information and for preparing plans of other Japanese prisons.

14. The only deviation from the Japanese pattern of building prisons on radial plans occurred after a disastrous fire damaged Hiroshima prison in 1883, prompting a shift of policy in favor of isolated parallel cellblocks. After five years this type of prison design was abandoned as too inconvenient, and radial plans were again used.

15. See, for example, Michael R. Dutton, *Policing and Punishment in China: From Patriarchy to "the People"* (Cambridge: Cambridge University Press, 1992), p. 158.

16. The figure of three hundred prisons influenced by Eastern State Penitentiary and its sister institution at Trenton encompasses only the prisons subsequently erected on the principle of a center structure with several radiating wings arranged to facilitate visual inspection. This number excludes prisons influenced by pre-Cherry Hill models but includes those built up to the present time that were secondarily influenced by prisons modeled after the Philadelphia, Trenton, or Pentonville institutions.

Chapter VI (pages 81–99)

For the twentieth-century history of Eastern State Penitentiary, the official and historiographical accounts in print are of more limited use than for the nineteenth century. Harry Elmer Barnes's *Evolution of Penology in Pennsylvania: A Study in American Social History*, published in 1927, deals with the public history and the governmental aspects of the prison's past more than with its social or physical history. Negley K. Teeters and John D. Shearer focused on the earlier years in *The Prison at Philadelphia, Cherry Hill: The Separate System of Penal Discipline, 1829–1913* (New York: Columbia University Press, 1957). By the 1930s the fact-filled annual reports of the Board of Inspectors (later Trustees) of the prison had ceased. And before the end of that decade the biennial reports of the Department of Welfare (which, beginning in the 1920s, replaced the annual reports of the Board of Public Charities) gave much less information about the prison at Cherry Hill. One must turn to various other sources, such as the newspaper clippings and photographs organized by topic in the morgues of *The Philadelphia Inquirer* and *The Evening Bulletin*, now at the Urban Archives at Temple University, Philadelphia. These have been gathered by Milton Marks, Director of the Eastern State Penitentiary Project of The Preservation Coalition of Greater Philadelphia. Also extremely useful are the oral histories collected and transcribed at the behest of the Eastern State Penitentiary Task Force. As yet tapped only in part are the manuscript records at the Pennsylvania State Archives, Harrisburg, particularly the "Warden's Daily Journal" and the "Monthly Minutes of the Board of Inspectors of Eastern State Penitentiary," excerpts from which have been provided to me by Richard Fullmer of Millersville State University. I am also grateful for insights shared by Norman Johnston, Finn Hornum of LaSalle University, Leslie C. Patrick-Stamp of Bucknell University, Michele Taylor of the University of Pennsylvania, David Cornelius of the Vitetta Group, Emma Jones Lapsansky of Haverford College, Marianna Thomas and Harry Bolick of Marianna Thomas Architects, Gretchen Worden of the Mütter Museum, and Daniel McCoubrey of Venturi, Scott Brown and Associates, Inc.

The official perspective is offered by annual reports that span more than a century and were published by four different governing bodies. The earliest were the annual reports of the penitentiary's Board of Inspectors, covering a calendar year and issued at the start of the following year. The first appeared in January 1830, covering activities for the year 1829, and was published in combination with the second in early 1831. These are referred to in this chapter as ESP, *Annual Report*, followed by the volume number and the year it appeared. These form an unbroken sequence from volume 1/2 (1831) to volume 44 (1873). The next published report, the forty-fifth, appeared in February 1875 and embraced two years. The sequence resumed from volume 46 (1876) to volume 91 (1921). Most were written by the penitentiary's principal officers, including the president of the board, the warden, the physician, and the moral instructor. They presented numerous case histories and statistical reports.

The series continued erratically after the Board of Inspectors was replaced by the Board of Trustees, who published annual reports from 1924 to 1929, unnumbered, at the end of May for the previous twelve months. These are referred to in this chapter as ESP, *Annual Report* (1924), to ESP, *Annual Report* (1929).

The series of annual reports by the Board of Public Charities began in 1871 and covered many institutions in addition to Eastern State Penitentiary. They were published regularly from the first, BPC, *Annual Report*, vol. 1 (1871), to BPC, *Annual Report*, vol. 48 (1918).

The Board of Public Charities was replaced in 1921 by the Department of Welfare, which published biennial reports from 1922. The first Department of Welfare biennial report is referred to here as DW, *Biennial Report*, vol. 1 (1922). These continued into the 1950s, but from the late 1930s were significantly less detailed about the penitentiary than previous annual reports.

1. The minutes of the Board of Trustees from early 1937 noted the appropriation of $25,000 for new gates and permission to reuse materials from the emergency hospital, built between cellblocks two and three in 1907–8. "Monthly Minutes of the Board of Trustees of Eastern State Penitentiary," January 14 and February 11, 1937, Pennsylvania State Archives, Harrisburg. Workmen replacing the old doors were photographed in 1937, and a view of the completed new front gateway appeared in the following year with the title "New Entrance for an Old Landmark." *The Evening Bulletin*, April 1, 1937, and November 2, 1938.

2. BPC, *Annual Report*, vol. 30 (1900).

3. ESP, *Annual Report*, vol. 67 (1897).

4. See Harry Elmer Barnes, *The Evolution of Penology in Pennsylvania: A Study in American Social History* (Indianapolis: Bobbs-Merrill, 1927), pp. 205, 249–55, 277–78.

5. Biographical notes on Vaux are given in ESP, *Annual Report*, vol. 59 (1889); BPC, *Annual Report*, vol. 22 (1892), and vol. 26 (1896); and Negley K. Teeters and John D. Shearer, *The Prison at Philadelphia, Cherry Hill: The Separate System of Penal Discipline, 1829–1913* (New York: Columbia University Press, 1957), pp. 91–92, 212–15. Accounts of Cassidy's career appear in ESP, *Annual Report*, vol. 71 (1901), and BPC, *Annual Report*, vol. 31 (1901). Cassidy's views on penology are given in his own words in *Warden Cassidy on Prisons and Convicts: Remarks from Observation and Experience Gained during Thirty-seven Years' Continuous Service in the Administration of the Eastern State Penitentiary, Pennsylvania* (Philadelphia: Patterson and White, 1897). Sketches of both men are also featured in Amos H. Mylin, comp., *State Prisons, Hospitals, Soldiers' Homes and Orphan Schools Controlled by the Commonwealth of Pennsylvania*, 2 vols. (n.p., 1897).

6. ESP, *Annual Report*, vol. 70 (1900).

7. A set of eight large drawings at the Historical Society of Pennsylvania, four of them dated 1900 but some clearly amended later, detail the state of the architectural fabric at the time and show the projected improvements.

William S. Vaux, Jr. (1872–1908) was a cousin of Richard Vaux. After Richard's death, William's elder brother George Vaux (1863–1927) was appointed one of the penitentiary's six inspectors, and served from 1898 to 1905. F. W. Leach, "Old Philadelphia Families: Vaux," *The North American* (Philadelphia), November 22, 1908.

8. ESP, *Annual Report*, vol. 70 (1900), to ESP, *Annual Report*, vol. 78 (1908).

9. BPC, *Annual Report*, vol. 33 (1903); "Monthly Minutes of the Board of Inspectors of Eastern State Penitentiary," October 3, 1903, Pennsylvania State Archives, Harrisburg.

10. ESP, *Annual Report*, vol. 88 (1918), p. 73, noted that the policy of issuing masks to new arrivals was discontinued in 1903 at the urging of Dr. Charles D. Hart of the Board of Inspectors.

11. BPC, *Annual Report*, vol. 11 (1881).

12. ESP, *Annual Report*, vol. 80 (1910), and vol. 82 (1912).

13. BPC, *Annual Report*, vol. 41 (1911).

14. ESP, *Annual Report*, vol. 83 (1913).

15. BPC, *Annual Report*, vol. 39 (1909), and vol. 40 (1910); Barnes, *Evolution of Penology*, 1927, pp. 205–6.

16. BPC, *Annual Report*, vol. 41 (1911); *Journal of House of Representatives of the Commonwealth of Pennsylvania* (Harrisburg, 1914), pt. 1, p. 65.

17. *Laws of the General Assembly of the Commonwealth of Pennsylvania Passed at the Session of 1913* (Harrisburg, Pennsylvania, 1913), pp. 708, 821.

18. ESP, *Annual Report*, vol. 84 (1914).

19. ESP, *Annual Report*, vol. 85 (1915).

20. BPC, *Annual Report*, vol. 44 (1914).

21. See Barnes, *Evolution of Penology*, 1927, pp. 229–30, 252–58. A newspaper story (*The Evening Ledger*, November 30, 1925) noted that independent work at the prison was "banishing idleness." About 300 of the 1,300 prisoners were working in the Department of Welfare's shops, but 700 more were in business for themselves or other inmates. They made model ships, beaded bags, parchment lampshades, fire screens, card tables, and radios. Some equipment for these hobby shops and marketing assistance were provided by Henry G. Brock, a former banker, who had been imprisoned at the penitentiary for killing three pedestrians with his car while intoxicated.

22. *Laws of the General Assembly of the Commonwealth of Pennsylvania Passed at the Session of 1921* (Harrisburg, Pennsylvania, 1921), pp. 1,144–59.

23. ESP, *Annual Report* (1924).

24. The architects were Zimmerman, Saxe and Zimmerman, of Chicago; the construction engineers were Day and Zimmerman, of Philadelphia. ESP, *Annual Report* (1925), (1927), and (1928); DW, *Biennial Report*, vol. 5 (1930), p. 55; and Barnes, *Evolution of Penology*, 1927, p. 206.

25. Board of Trustees of Eastern State Penitentiary, "6th Biennial Report," June 1, 1930, to May 31, 1932, Pennsylvania State Archives, Harrisburg; *The Philadelphia Inquirer*, December 19, 1933; and "Warden's Daily Journal," October 1, 1936, Pennsylvania State Archives, Harrisburg.

26. See Barnes, *Evolution of Penology*, 1927, p. 206.

27. ESP, *Annual Report* (1926), and (1927); *The Philadelphia Inquirer*, August 17, 1926.

28. Barnes, *Evolution of Penology*, 1927, pp. 229–32, 251–58; ESP, *Annual Report* (1925). Quoted passages in ESP, *Annual Report*, vol. 91 (1921).

29. Barnes, *Evolution of Penology*, 1927, pp. 302–3.

30. Issues of *The Umpire*, dated March 19 to December 13, 1913, courtesy of Richard Fullmer of Millersville State University.

31. ESP, *Annual Report* (1924), and (1925). Teeters and Shearer (*Cherry Hill*, 1957, p. 223) reported that the last female prisoner was removed on December 12, 1923.

32. ESP, *Annual Report*, vol. 88 (1918).

33. ESP, *Annual Report*, vol. 90 (1920).

34. *The Philadelphia Inquirer*, July 22, 1934; Oral History Project for the Eastern State Penitentiary Task Force (hereafter cited as ESP Oral History Project), interview with Joseph R. Brierly.

35. *The Philadelphia Inquirer*, August 17, 1926; *The Evening Ledger*, February 15, 1928, and September 19, 1931; *The Philadelphia Record*, August 15, 1931; and ESP Oral History Project, interview with Joseph R. Brierly.

36. *The Philadelphia Inquirer*, July 15, 16, 17, and 18, 1923, January 3, 1925, July 22, 1934, and February 15, 1940; ESP, *Annual Report* (1924), (1926), and (1927); *The Philadelphia Record*, February 15, 1940; and *The Evening Bulletin*, July 14, 16, and 17, 1923, January 2, 1925, and April 4, 1945.

37. ESP, *Annual Report* (1924); *The Evening Bulletin*, September 6, 1923.

38. *The Philadelphia Inquirer*, May 29 and 30, 1924.

39. *The Philadelphia Inquirer*, May 29 and 30, 1924.

40. The major escape attempts provided newspapers with occasions for reviewing earlier ones. *The Philadelphia Inquirer*, January 3, 1925, July 23, 1926, December 19, 1933, July 22, August 29, September 1, 1934, November 4, 1939, February 15,

1940, March 22, 1942, December 7, 1944, April 4, October 22, 1945, and January 9, 1961; *The Evening Bulletin*, January 2, 1925, November 21, 1933, and October 27, 1943; and *The Philadelphia Record*, February 15, 1940, March 24, 1942, and April 4, 1945. See also ESP, *Annual Report* (1927), and (1928); Commonwealth of Pennsylvania, Department of Welfare, *Prison Report, Department of Welfare: A Review of the Four-Year Period, 1931–34 Inclusive, in the Penal and Correctional Institutions of the Commonwealth and a Discussion of Objectives*, special issue, no. 62 (Harrisburg, 1935); and "Monthly Minutes of the Board of Trustees of Eastern State Penitentiary," October 11, 1934, and December 5, 1938, Pennsylvania State Archives, Harrisburg. The April 1945 escape received extensive newspaper coverage, with diagrams and photographs. A summary by Seymour Shubin, titled "Breaking Out Is Hard to Do," appeared in *Philadelphia Magazine* (August 1990), pp. 147ff.

41. Department of Welfare, *Prison Report*, 1935; "Monthly Minutes of the Board of Trustees of Eastern State Penitentiary," April 9, 1936, Pennsylvania State Archives, Harrisburg.

42. Department of Welfare, *Prison Report*, 1935; *The Philadelphia Inquirer*, December 19, 1933, and March 9, 1938; and ESP Oral History Project, interview with Joseph R. Brierly.

43. Several dozen interviews conducted with former wardens, guards, inmates, and neighbors recall the past several decades, back to the 1920s in some cases. These have been collected and transcribed by the ESP Oral History Project.

44. Board of Trustees of Eastern State Penitentiary, "6th Biennial Report," June 1, 1930, to May 31, 1932, Pennsylvania State Archives, Harrisburg; ESP Oral History Project, interview with "H.B."

45. *The Evening Ledger*, March 24, 1933; *The Philadelphia Inquirer*, December 19, 1933; Department of Welfare, *Prison Report*, 1935; *The Philadelphia Record*, December 23, 1941; and *The Evening Bulletin*, March 29, 1943.

46. *The Evening Bulletin*, March 29, September 1, 1943, and June 18, 1945; Harry Elmer Barnes, Negley K. Teeters, and A. G. Fraser for the Institute of Local Government, Pennsylvania State College, *Report on Penal and Correctional Institutions and Correctional Policy in the State of Pennsylvania* (State College: Pennsylvania State College, 1944), pp. 12–13; and *The Philadelphia Record*, March 26, June 18, August 3, and November 8, 1945. The peg-making enterprise, run by four "capitalists" serving life sentences, reportedly earned $58,300 in two years and employed fifty inmates.

47. *The Philadelphia Record*, December 23, 1941, and October 15, 1942; *The Evening Bulletin*, September 1, 1943; and *The Philadelphia Inquirer*, September 7 and November 21, 1943.

48. *The Philadelphia Record*, February 19, 1928; *The Philadelphia Inquirer*, February 19, 1928, and October 25, 1939; *The Evening Bulletin*, May 8, 1934; Department of Welfare, *Prison Report*, 1935; and ESP Oral History Project, interview with Joseph R. Brierly.

49. *The Philadelphia Inquirer*, September 1, 1934; *The Evening Ledger*, September 1, 1938; and ESP Oral History Project, interview with Joseph R. Brierly.

50. *The Evening Ledger*, December 13, 1925; *The Evening Bulletin*, February 28, 1941; and ESP Oral History Project, interview with "H.B."

51. *The Evening Ledger*, October 1, 1934, April 28, and May 13, 1936; *The Philadelphia Inquirer*, April 25, 1938, February 5, 1940, November 2, 1942, October 9, December 7, 1944, October 24, 1945, and May 18, 1946; and *The Philadelphia Record*, February 15, 1940, and December 7, 1944.

52. *The Philadelphia Record*, February 8, 1934.

53. ESP Oral History Project, interviews with "H.B.," Joseph R. Brierly, Richard Parcell, and Charles Williams. An unidentified clipping from a 1934 newspaper noted the elimination that year of a predecessor, the "blackjack squad."

54. *The Evening Ledger*, March 24, 1933.

55. *The Evening Ledger*, March 24, 1933; *The Philadelphia Inquirer*, December 19, 1933. The resulting population of over 3,000 inmates would be far greater than what Smith thought proper for "individual treatment," since a warden could not know his men individually when their number rose above about 1,200. Nevertheless, he felt that the different cellblocks at Graterford could function completely separately, each with its own dining hall and shop, obviating that problem. In their 1944 *Report on Penal and Correctional Institutions* (p. 10), Barnes, Teeters and Fraser called Warden Smith "a good disciplinarian," but found him "not too sympathetic with some of the newer approaches to rehabilitation."

56. Department of Welfare, *Prison Report*, 1935; "Monthly Minutes of the Board of Trustees of Eastern State Penitentiary," October 11, 1934, Pennsylvania State Archives, Harrisburg; and "Warden's Daily Journal," April 30, 1941, Pennsylvania State Archives, Harrisburg. Nonetheless, only a "skeleton classification clinic," meeting weekly, operated as late as 1943, and rehabilitative efforts were limited. Barnes, Teeters, and Fraser, *Report on Penal and Correctional Institutions*, 1944, p. 11.

57. Barnes, Teeters, and Fraser, *Report on Penal and Correctional Institutions*, 1944, p. 10.

58. Barnes, Teeters, and Fraser, *Report on Penal and Correctional Institutions*, 1944, pp. 9–10.

59. *The Philadelphia Inquirer*, July 9, 1944; *The Philadelphia Record*, July 11, 1944.

60. *The Philadelphia Record*, March 27, 1945.

61. *The Philadelphia Inquirer*, May 1, 1945.

62. Barnes, Teeters, and Fraser, *Report on Penal and Correctional Institutions*, 1944, p. 10.

63. *The Evening Bulletin*, March 6, 1946.

64. *The Evening Bulletin*, February 26, 1946; *The Philadelphia Daily News*, March 11, 1947.

65. Department of Justice, State of Pennsylvania, Bureau of Correction, *Eastern Correctional Diagnostic and Classification Center, Philadelphia, Pennsylvania* (Philadelphia: Department of Justice, 1954), foreword.

66. Bureau of Correction, *Eastern Correctional Diagnostic and Classification Center*, 1954, pp. 5–6, 20–22; *The Evening Bulletin*, May 19, 1954.

67. The effort seems to have been spurred by the collapse of a roof in the hospital block in November 1951, but some of the blueprints for the changes (at the Philadelphia Historical Commission) are dated as early as February 1950. Bureau of Correction, *Eastern Correctional Diagnostic and Classification Center*, 1954, pp. 12, 21; *The Evening Bulletin*, June 8, 1952; and ESP Oral History Project, interview with "H.B."

68. *The Evening Bulletin*, June 8, 1952; "Warden's Daily Journal," March 31 and June 17, 1959, Pennsylvania State Archives, Harrisburg; and Bureau of Correction, *Eastern Correctional Diagnostic and Classification Center*, 1954, pp. 5–6. A cost estimate (dated October 7, 1953) for a chapel and auditorium at Eastern State Penitentiary by James A. Nolen, architect, and W. H. Swinburne, associate, and a preliminary design for the same (dated October 28, 1960) by Dagit Associates (Albert F. Dagit) are among the papers found at the penitentiary and deposited at the Philadelphia Historical Commission. Blueprints of working drawings of the expanded visiting room by Keast & Hemphill (dated January 18, 1962) are also at the Philadelphia Historical Commission.

69. ESP Oral History Project, interviews with "H.B." and Joseph R. Brierly; *The Philadelphia Inquirer*, October 12, 1958; and *The Evening Bulletin*, March 25, 1958, and May 15, 1960.

70. *The Philadelphia Inquirer*, October 12, 1958.

71. ESP Oral History Project, interview with Joseph R. Brierly; *The Philadelphia Inquirer*, October 12, 1958.

72. *The Philadelphia Inquirer*, January 9 and 10, and February 12, 1961; *The Philadelphia Daily News*, January 12, 1961; and ESP Oral History Project, interview with Joseph R. Brierly.

73. *The Philadelphia Inquirer*, January 11, 1965.

74. *The Philadelphia Inquirer*, March 29, August 24, 1962, January 11, and April 27, 1965; *The Evening Bulletin*, July 22, 1962.

75. *The Philadelphia Inquirer*, July 12, 1967, December 15, 1968, August 31, 1969, and January 28, 1970.

76. *Progress Report and Proposed Program Development of the Eastern Correctional Diagnostic and Classification Center and State Correctional Institution at Philadelphia or Its Replacement Facility*, October 1, 1968; ESP Oral History Project, interview with Joseph R. Brierly.

77. ESP Oral History Project, interview with Joseph R. Brierly. The transcript identifies the commissioner as Arthur Guarachi; this was presumably Prasse, still commissioner in 1969. *The Philadelphia Inquirer*, September 11, 1969; *The Philadelphia Daily News*, September 10, 1969.

78. *The Evening Bulletin*, June 4, 1970; *The Philadelphia Inquirer*, July 2, 6, and 10, November 28, 1970, and June 24, 1980; and *The Philadelphia Daily News*, January 2, 1971.

79. *The Philadelphia Inquirer*, June 2, 1984.

80. *The Philadelphia Inquirer*, May 29 and 30, 1974, March 8, 1981, and June 2, 1984; Richard J. Webster, *Philadelphia Preserved: Catalog of the Historic American Building Survey*, 2nd ed. (Philadelphia: Temple University Press, 1981), pp. 295–96. The story of the various redevelopment efforts in the 1970s and 1980s is told in Dennis R. Montagna, "Philadelphia's Eastern State Penitentiary: These Stone Walls Do Not a Shopping Center Make," in Lynda H. Schneekloth, Marcia F. Feuerstein, and Barbara A. Campagna, eds., *Changing Places: ReMaking Institutional Buildings* (Fredonia, New York: White Pine Press, 1992), pp. 258–80.

81. Norman B. Johnston, "The Development of Radial Prisons: A Case Study in Cultural Diffusion," Ph.D. diss., University of Pennsylvania, 1958; Matthew Eli Baigell, "John Haviland," Ph.D. diss., University of Pennsylvania, 1965; Negley K. Teeters, *They Were in Prison: A History of the Pennsylvania Prison Society, 1787–1937 . . .* (Philadelphia: John C. Winston, 1937); Teeters, *The Cradle of the Penitentiary: The Walnut Street Jail at Philadelphia, 1773–1835* (Philadelphia: Pennsylvania Prison Society, 1955); and David J. Rothman, *The Discovery of the Asylum: Social Order and Disorder in the New Republic* (Boston: Little, Brown, 1971).

Chapter VII (pages 101—5)

1. Such prison units or separate prisons have been established or are being planned in over thirty states, including California, Arizona, Colorado, Connecticut, Minnesota, Wisconsin, New York, and Pennsylvania. Pennsylvania, for example, has a Special Management Unit at Camp Hill. Prisoners are locked in their cells all but forty-five minutes a day. They exercise in a cage outside their cells and are allowed one religious book and a box for their legal papers in their cells. They can receive one approved, one-hour visit from a family member every month. No magazines, radio, or television are allowed. Work or educational programs are nonexistent. Prisoners are not allowed to mingle with other prisoners.

2. Stun guns fire a dart attached to an electrical wire that delivers a brief charge of 50,000 volts at low amperage, resulting in the temporary immobilization of the targeted individual.

3. For more on the prisons at Pelican Bay, California, and Marion, Illinois, see J. M. Olivero and James Roberts, "The U.S. Federal Penitentiary at Marion, Illinois: Alcatraz Revisited," *New England Journal on Criminal and Civil Confinement*, vol. 16 (Winter 1990), pp. 21–51; Russ Immarigeon, "The Marionization of American Prisons," *National Prison Project Journal*, vol. 7 (Fall 1992), pp. 1–5; Jan Elvin, "Isolation, Excessive Force under Attack at California's Supermax," *National Prison Project Journal*, vol. 7 (Fall 1992), pp. 5, 21–22; John Ross, "High-Tech Dungeon," *The Bay Guardian*, September 23, 1992, pp. 15–16; and "Suit Alleges Violations in California's 'Super-Max' Prison," *Criminal Justice Newsletter*, September 1, 1993, pp. 2–3. A "60 Minutes" segment, titled "Pelican Bay," was produced for CBS television by Lowell Bergman with Mike Wallace as interviewer and aired in the fall of 1993. Details of punishing prisoners by hog-tying are described in the official newspaper for the U.S. District Court for Northern California, *The Recorder*. See Howard Mintz, "Is Pelican Bay Too Tough?" *The Recorder*, September 19, 1991, p. 8.

4. Studies are cited in Stuart Grassian and Nancy Friedman, "Effects of Sensory Deprivation in Psychiatric Seclusion and Solitary Confinement," *International Journal of Law and Psychiatry*, vol. 8 (1986), p. 49. See also statements made by Dr. Grassian in Mike Wallace's interview on "60 Minutes" (Fall 1993). Dr. Grassian has studied SHU inmates at a number of locations, including a facility for women at Bedford Hills, New York. "Many became grossly disorganized and psychotic, smearing themselves with feces, mumbling and screaming incoherently all day and night, some even descending to the horror of eating parts of their own bodies." Stuart Grassian, "Amended Declaration," *Madrid v. Gomez*, U.S. District Court for Northern California, 1993, p. 166.

5. Max Grünhut, *Penal Reform, A Comparative Study* (Oxford: Clarendon Press, 1948), p. 131.

6. The prisons were respectively: Mills's Burlington County Jail, New Jersey (1808); Latrobe's Virginia Penitentiary, Richmond (1797–1800); Strickland's first Western Penitentiary, near Pittsburgh (1826); Bulfinch's Massachusetts State Prison, Charlestown (1805); and Dance's Newgate Prison, London (1770–85).

7. Henry-Russell Hitchcock, *Early Victorian Architecture in Britain* (New Haven, Connecticut: Yale University Press, 1954), vol. 1, p. 191.

8. Sanford Bates, former director of the Federal Bureau of Prisons, visited European prisons in the decade prior to World War II and in 1936 wrote: "In France, Holland, Italy, and other countries of western Europe, solitary or separate confinement is the rule. The prisoner lives alone, works alone, eats by himself, and even takes his exercise and his religion literally in solitude. In many prisons in Europe no convict ever sees the face of a single one of his fellow prisoners. On the rare occasions on which he does leave his cell he wears a mask or head covering." Sanford Bates, *Prisons and Beyond* (New York: Macmillan, 1936), p. 85. See also Norman S. Hayner, "German Correctional Procedures: Impact of the Occupation," *National Probation and Parole Association Journal*, vol. 1, no. 2 (October 1955), p. 172.

9. For a discussion of these issues see David J. Rothman, *The Discovery of the Asylum: Social Order and Disorder in the New Republic* (Boston: Little, Brown, 1971).